The Scottish Terrier

POPULAR DOGS' BREED SERIES

THE SCOTTISH TERRIER

DOROTHY CASPERSZ

Revised by Elizabeth Meyer

Arco Publishing Company Inc.

New York

Published in the United States
by Arco Publishing Company Inc.,
219 Park Avenue South
New York, N.Y. 10003

First published (as *The Popular Scottish Terrier*) 1956
Second edition, revised 1962
Third edition, revised (as *The Scottish Terrier*) 1976
Second edition, revised © T. W. L. Caspersz 1962
Revisions to third edition © Estate of T. W. L. Caspersz 1976

Printed in Great Britain

Library of Congress Cataloging in Publication Data

Caspersz, Dorothy.
   The Scottish terrier.

   First (1956)– 2nd (1962) ed. published under title:
The popular Scottish terrier.
   Bibliography: p.
   Includes index.
   1. Scottish terriers. I. Title.

SF429.S4C   1976b   636.7'55   76-25803
ISBN 0-668-04060-2 (Cloth Edition)

Dedicated to the memory of
TURFIELD BOTTLE OF INK (BOI)
May 23, 1937 – September 23, 1951

To know, to esteem, to love – and then to part
Makes up life's tale to many a feeling heart.

COLERIDGE

CONTENTS

ILLUSTRATIONS

Int. Ch. Walsing Winning Trick
Bred and owned by Mr. W. M. Singleton
Ch. Niddbank Blue Print
Bred and owned by Mrs. K. M. Ross
Ch. Ortley Simon
Bred and owned by Dr. C. Bremer
Ch. Westpark Rio Grande *Bred and owned by Mr. A. H. Jones*

Between pages 96 and 97

Ch. Gosmore Eilburn Admaration
Bred by Mrs. M. Punton
Owned by Mr. and Mrs. C. Pillsbury
Ch. Ortley Sandy
Bred and owned by Dr. C. Bremer
Ch. Gosmore Eilburn Miss Hopeful
Bred by Mrs. M. Punton
Owned by Mrs. A. B. Dallison
Ch. Niddbank Miss Blue Print
Bred by Dr. C. Flintoff
Owned by Mrs. K. M. Ross
Ch. Gaywyn Wicked Lady
Bred by Mrs. A. B. Dallison
Owned by Mrs. M. Owen
Ch. Kennelgarth Viking; his dam, Ch. Kennelgarth Gleam,
    and his sire, Ch. Kennelgarth Eros
All owned by Miss B. Penn-Bull
Ch. Medwal Wild Oats
Bred by Messrs Medcalf and Pease
Owned by Mr. W. Medcalf
Ch. Westpark Derriford Baffie
Bred by Mr. F. Andrews
Owned by Mr. A. H. James
Ch. Glenview Guardsman
Bred and owned by Mr. A. H. Gee
Ch. Con of Conett
Bred by Mr. A. H. Hanson
Owned by Messrs Gill and Moore

Between pages 128 and 129

Ch. Reanda Roger Rough
Bred and owned by Mrs. E. Meyer
Ch. Gaywyn Kingson
Bred and owned by Mrs. M. Owen
Kennelgarth family group
Owned by Miss B. Penn-Bull
Ch. Bidfield Bix
Bred and owned by the Misses Payne and Harrold

Between pages 128 and 129

Ch. Glenview Sir Galahad
Bred and owned by Mr. A. H. Gee

Int. Ch. Wyrebury Wrangler
Bred and owned by Mr. W. Berry

Ch. Gaywyn Likely Lad
Bred and owned by Mrs. M. Owen

Ch. Viewpark Pilot
Bred and owned by Mr. A. N. Maclaren

IN THE TEXT

Silhouette line drawings

Author's Introduction

IT is my belief that nine people out of ten never read the preface to a book. If they do, what do they expect to find in it? After having striven to write a book on the subject nearest one's heart, it seems to me the most difficult task is to compile for it a preface. As in this case it is being attempted after the various chapters for the book were finished, it would seem its position should be at the end rather than the beginning. However, one must assume part of its purpose is to introduce either the author or the book, or both, to the reader, so I will endeavour to do just that.

History relates that it was in 1894 that I first became the nominal owner of that thing of courage and charm, mystery and magnetism, a Scottish Terrier, though blissfully unconscious at the time of the benefit thus conferred upon me. Memory denies any clear recollection of the little bitch (for she was but a sixteen-pounder when matured), protector and playmate of my childhood, until she and I were both six years old, when she bred a litter of puppies. One of these maintained the family tradition of a Scot in the home for fourteen more years, a home which, I am thankful to say, has never since been without one or more of these unique personalities.

Early recollections can be very boring, but one I feel is worth recording for its instructive value. The puppy retained from the original bitch was taken one day to be shown to her breeder, who put the memorable query 'Can it run?' There is more in this than may at first appear, for this breeder – one of the early pioneers in the breed – was no doubt well aware that freedom of movement and agility were ever essential to the make-up of a Scottish Terrier. The judge of today does not use the phrase 'Can it run?' but he requires that it shall be able to 'run' nevertheless.

It is true to say that all the best contacts, friendships, and experiences in my life have been due, directly or indirectly, to Scottish Terriers, and if this book gives any pleasure or guidance to others who are, or who become, interested in the breed, I would like to feel that it represents the measure of my deep gratitude to those in the past who gave me of their knowledge when I took up breeding and exhibiting in all seriousness.

It was in 1907, at Abergavenny, under the late famous all-rounder judge George Raper, that I made my first hesitant venture into a show-ring and received a well-deserved rebuke in the never-forgotten words: 'Lead him on the other side, little girl; it's the dog I want to see, not you.' About that time Mr. McCanlish gave me a good bitch on breeding terms, and Mr. Ludlow (founder of the S.T.C.E.) bought from me the first pups I bred. My kennel was thus well and truly started, but being still at school and later taking up physical training as a profession, much of the care of the young stock devolved upon my mother. She came of a Staffordshire family, breeders of horses and dogs for many generations, and there was no one better at raising and educating puppies, so I was lucky. Subsequently marrying a dog lover, who proceeded in a short space of time and with effortless ease to go bang to the top in Cairn Terriers, again I was lucky, for no one could have proved more tolerant, sympathetic, and encouraging towards a wife's all-absorbing interest in dogs, than my partner in life's joys and sorrows has been. Himself also an accepted judge of our breed, his drive and enthusiasm has many a time spurred me on to fresh hope and renewed effort in connection with the dogs, and this seems a fitting opportunity to place on record my indebtedness.

Thirteen years' apprenticeship as an exhibitor, during which period I encountered most of the pitfalls to which the novice is ever prone, led up to my first judging engagement, which was at the Championship show of the Ladies Kennel Association in 1920. How much more fortunate are the new judges of today, who usually enjoy a few 'dummy-runs' at minor shows before undertaking the responsible task of handing out Challenge Certificates!

So much for the author. Now we are more or less acquainted, let me outline briefly the aims of this book. In my capacity as correspondent to one of the canine papers and as secretary of a breed Club, it is only natural that a lot of queries from beginners have come my way through the years. They ask the oddest questions, but the recurring grumble seems to be that none of the books they can find on the breed contain enough information on one point or another.

Consequently, when asked to write this book I said to myself it must not only cover the same ground as previous books on the breed but a good deal more besides, including the various details the novice wants to know. My aim has been to deal with everything, so far as I see it, which pertains to the keeping of Scottish Terriers. There is always more to be learnt about any subject, and if there are still any serious omissions in the chapters which follow I beg the readers forgiveness in advance.

The practical recommendations throughout are based on personal experience, and here I would remind anyone contemplating taking up the breed either as a hobby or a business, of the old adage: 'If you want a thing done well, do it yourself.' No motto pays the dog owner better dividends than this. Do the work yourself, whether it be scrubbing kennel floors, washing sheep's paunches, or sitting up all night with a sick dog or a whelping bitch. Only this way can you know if the dogs are properly cared for. Only this way can you gain the greatest enjoyment from them. Also it is an effective remedy against keeping too many. You have either bought them or caused them to be born into this world in the first place, therefore the responsibility for their welfare and happiness is yours alone.

In this book I have tried to stress the desirability of building up a strain of one's own. There is no limit to the absorbing interest resulting from the ownership of many successive generations all from the same original stock. Apart from physical features, the inherited traits of character and behaviour provide a wealth of entertainment, and if any of my readers happen to be keen gardeners they will appreciate that there is a similarity between cultivating one's own plot of ground over a long period and developing one's own family of dogs. In both cases one selects, one discards, one reorganizes, till eventually there is a garden or a race of animals reflecting one's own personality, the response and reactions from which one can anticipate and recognize. I can think of no better wish, therefore, to all who set out to cultivate the Scottish Terrier, than that, like a garden that is loved, it may be fitted to serve its original purpose, be practical and healthy, have a well-cared-for appearance and be withal a thing of beauty.

August 1955   D.S.C.

Author's Introduction

SINCE this book first appeared in 1956, I think perhaps the most noteworthy developments in our breed during the past five years have been: first, the astounding number of Champions bearing the Reanda prefix which have been made in this period, and secondly, the proportion of owner-handled exhibits which have attained top honours in the show-ring as compared to those handled by professionals. From 1956 to 1960 inclusive, sixty new British champions have qualified, thirty-three of which have been owner-prepared and handled. This proportion works out similarly when reviewing Challenge Certificate winners, all of which do not necessarily finish Champions, for, of the fifty or so Certificates on offer each year, 50 per cent have been won by exhibits prepared and handled to victory by their owners. This I consider is a most healthy sign, for one has only to look around at certain other breeds, the show winners in which are almost exclusively in the hands of professionals, to realize how lamentably such breeds have lost popularity.

So long as we can number among our breeders and exhibitors those who have the patience and perseverance to emulate the skill of the professional handlers in the matter of coat preparation and ring-craft, so long will the general popularity of the unique Diehard be maintained. The main opportunity offered to the general public of assessing the behaviour and characteristics of the various breeds is by attendance at dog shows, and the owner-handled winners, which have in the main been loved and understood from puppyhood onwards, can make a stronger appeal to the average onlooker than the professionally handled exhibits propped up both ends and devoid of individuality.

August 1961   D. S.C.

Reviser's Note

TO THE THIRD EDITION

DOROTHY CASPERSZ died suddenly in October 1961 not long before the second edition of this book appeared. Her husband, T. W. L. Caspersz, assisted with the proofs of that edition and subsequently watched over the fortunes of *The Popular Scottish Terrier*, as the book was then known. Sadly, he too has now died, and the publishers have invited me to bring the third edition up to date. I have, with some diffidence, tried to undertake this task – and perhaps it is hardly surprising, when one remembers Mrs. Caspersz' lifelong devotion to the breed and her record as a Scottish Terrier breeder and judge, that very few revisions are required to the substance of her text. Mrs. Caspersz' introductions to the first and second editions are still included as they indicate so clearly her reasons for writing the book and the forthright – and, I think, still valid – opinions which she held about the breed.

My main work has been concentrated on bringing the chapters on Families, Breeding, and Puppy-rearing up to date and on largely rewriting the final chapter on Ailments. I must however mention in this Note the names of a few of the number of Scottish Terriers who have achieved fame in the last twenty-five years, through going Best in Show All Breeds at Championship Shows, or winning a record number of Challenge Certificates, or by having made a special impact on the breed by siring a record number of champions. Their names are found in many pedigrees of today and therefore have had a great influence on the breed. Such dogs – to list only a few – are: Ch. Kennelgarth Viking, Int. Ch. Bardene Bingo, Ch. Reanda Roger Rough, Int. Ch. Gosmore Eilburn Admaration, Ch. Gaywyn Viscountess, Ch. Gillsie Highland Lass, Ch. Gosmore Eilburn Miss Hopeful, Ch. Reanda Ringold, Ch. Brio Jezebel, Ch. Brio Wishbone, Ch. Gosmore Gillsie Scotch Lad, Ch. Viewpart Anna, Ch. Brio Checkmate and last, but not least, the newest arrival to win Best in Show, Ch. Gaywyn Likely Lad.

I have also replaced a few of the photographs and augmented the appendices. The list of champions in Appendix C has been supplied by the Kennel Club, and I am grateful to Mr. Philip Cockrill, honorary secretary of the Scottish Terrier Breeders and Exhibitors Association, for his help in collating the details given in Appendices A, B, and D.

1976   E.M.

I

Origin

THAT the Scottish Terrier descends directly from a race of small terriers of great antiquity there is no shadow of doubt. What is probably the earliest known reference to the breed by name, occurs in the book *Recreations in Natural History*, published in 1815, wherein allusion is made to a 'wiry-haired Scotch Terrier' owned by Major-General Bonham, Governor of Surinam.

In 1837, the first published description of the breed was to be found in Thomas Bell's *A History of British Quadrupeds*. In this work it was stated there were at that time in Great Britain only two distinct varieties of Terrier: 'the one smooth, sleek, usually black and tan in colour . . . the other is called the Scottish or Wire-haired Terrier and it differs from the former in the rough harsh character of the hair, the shortness of the muzzle, the shortness and stoutness of the limbs, and the colour, which is generally dirty white, though they vary greatly in this respect.'

Two years later, two books on dogs were published, generally recorded as Charles Hamilton Smith's *Dogs, 1839–40*; the first dealing with wild dogs and the second principally with domestic dogs. In this latter there is given a description of the 'Wire-haired or Scottish Terrier'. Having referred to the two existing types of terrier in much the same terms as Thomas Bell, the author first describes the smooth-coated elegant terriers and continues: 'but the second is the more ancient and genuine breed, usually called the Wire-haired or Scottish Terrier; the muzzle is shorter and fuller, the limbs more stout, the fur hard and shaggy, and the colour a pale sandy or ochre, and sometimes white.'

A book published in 1847, called *Dogs, their Origin and Varieties*, by H. D. Richardson, contains the following reference to terriers of Scotland: 'There are two varieties of the common Scotch Terrier. One which stands rather high on his legs, usually of a sandy red colour, very strongly made and is commonly called the

Highland Terrier.' The other variety described obviously refers to the Dandie Dinmont.

In the book *Dogs of the British Isles*, by Stonehenge, published in 1867, there occur phrases in the chapter on 'Terriers, not being Skyes, Dandies, Fox or Toy' which seems distinctly applicable to our breed. We read: 'they are rough-headed and lion-hearted. The broken-haired terrier has a rough profile, but is not a thick-coated dog, the muzzle and eyebrows generally showing most fringe. The texture of the whole body is hairy and hard.'

It is on record that for some hundreds of years a breed of terrier with a rough coat had been kept in the Western Highlands of Scotland and the Hebrides. As he was bred for work, no general attempt would be made to breed him to one type. He would be selected for his working ability, his pluck and stamina, and as travel was a big undertaking in the fastnesses of the Highlands in those days, intermingling of strains was very improbable. Consequently several different types were evolved, due probably to personal preference. The Macdonalds of Skye evidently preferred the longer-coated and longer-bodied dogs, hence the development which led by selection to the Skye Terrier. The Malcolms of Poltalloch liked a small dog with short head, and later, having a family preference for cream-coloured or white dogs, cultivated what ultimately became the West Highland White Terrier. The Skye Terrier, the West Highland White, the Cairn, and quite probably the Yorkshire too, are all descended from the same original source. The breed now known as the Cairn Terrier made a sudden rise to popularity and the show bench about 1909, and though there is much difference of opinion as to his exact origin, for it is as much lost in the mists of antiquity as that of the other three breeds mentioned, we can safely assume that their origin is a common one. Just which of the varieties which came from a common progenitor most resembles that progenitor, it is at this stage impossible to tell, but it may be held with considerable assurance that the modern Scottish Terrier is directly descended from an ancient breed of dog which in general had most of the attributes we look for today.

The type from which our modern Scottish Terrier has been evolved was probably domiciled in the Blackmount region of Perthshire, the Moor of Rannoch, and surrounding districts. In Mr. Thomson Gray's monograph of the breed, *The Dogs of*

Scotland, published in 1887, an account is given of a driving tour
taken by a Captain Mackie about the year 1880. Captain Mackie
had a strong kennel of Scottish Terriers in the early days of their
show history. He tells of visiting several fox-hunters and tod-
hunters who had possessed the same strains for from forty to
sixty years, and dogs he bought on this tour are among those
which went to found our existing breed. Many of the details re-
counted by Captain Mackie are of interest. One of the first tod-
hunters he visited was one Robinson of Lochlomondside, who had
kept terriers for sixty years. His dogs stood about the height of the
modern Fox-terrier. Their coats were a bit open and rough
looking, but harsh. They had foxy-looking heads, semi-erect ears
and gaily carried tails. In colour they were a sort of rusty grey,
and each had one or more white feet. Robinson explained the
latter peculiarity by saying he had some twenty or thirty years
previously got a particularly game terrier from McCorkindale of
Hell's Glen. He liked this dog so well that he had used it much for
breeding, and always valued the puppies with white feet. The
weight of his terriers was from 17 lb. to 20 lb. It was recorded that
in Argyll they were mostly of a sandy colour with one ear up and
one down, while in Perthshire they were of all colours but a rusty
grey or pepper and salt predominated. The next visit was paid to
Donald Malloch, a keeper of the old sort who had seven or eight
good terriers. They were of various colours, from grizzly brindle
to sandy, weighing from 17 lb. to 20 lb., with big heads, strong
jaws and very big teeth, and ears that were semi-erect. The faults
Captain Mackie noted in them were the ears being heavy and the
tails inclined to curl. Mr. MacDonald's kennel at Blackmount
was visited, where terriers had been kept from time immemorial.
Here we learn that the short-legged cobby little dogs, weighing
about 19 lb., had long sharp muzzles, small eyes protected by
heavy eyebrows, and were of various sandy shades of colour. The
next call was made on Donald Cameron, fox-hunter of Glenorchy,
who brought out a batch of terriers of divers shapes, sizes and
colours. The prevailing colour, however, seems to have been
fawn, or sandy, and others were of the different shades of brindle.
Many of them had white chests, some had white feet, but of
whichever colour their coats were described as hard and wiry.

Enough has been said to show the antiquity of the stock from
which our breed originated. Points of special interest, in the light

of later developments, are the repeated references in these early records to big heads, harsh coats and light colours. It says much for the weight of long inheritance that the basic characteristics have prevailed throughout the past century. In spite of the probable haphazard breeding in the early days, in spite of later attempts by exhibitors to re-fashion the Scot into something merely ornamental, the main traits persist – the hardihood, the terrier instincts for going to ground and for killing vermin, the big head for the size of the dog, and the harsh coat.

2

History (Mainly Male)

IT was in the year 1879 that the Scottish Terrier as a distinct variety first appeared on the show bench. Prior to that a few entries had been made in classes provided for 'Scotch terriers of all Kinds', but we have no proof that any of those exhibited bore any resemblance to the Scottish Terrier as later recognized.

The first mention of the breed in the Kennel Club Stud Book describes it as 'Scotch or Broken-haired Terrier'. The name Scottish Terrier had at that time no definite breed attached to it, and the breed had no definite name, being variously alluded to as Highland, or Cairn, or Diehard. Then for a time it became known as the Aberdeen Terrier. It is nothing short of amazing how this old name of Aberdeen has clung, and indeed clings to this day. Though no class for Aberdeen Terriers has ever been provided at any show for at least seventy years, one still occasionally meets with enquiries for an Aberdeen Terrier from people who appear to think the Scottish Terrier is one breed and the Aberdeen another. They are very hard to convince that such is not, and never was the case. No doubt the main cause of the name Aberdeen lay in the fact that many of the earliest dogs to be shown were bred or owned in that town, notably the terriers belonging to Mr. J. A. Adamson. He was among the first to exhibit Scottish Terriers when in 1879 they were classified as a distinct breed.

The breed at that time was mainly in the hands of Scotsmen. Any Scottish Terrier south of the Border was a rare sight, and one can well imagine the interest aroused when in London, in 1879 at the Kennel Club show held in the Alexandra Palace, the first classes given for the breed resulted in thirteen entries. The judge was Mr. J. B. Morrison, of Greenock, one who had devoted much study to the breed in its early days and who was partly responsible for the first standard of the breed ever published. The winners on this occasion included a dog named Tartan and a bitch called Splinter II. Tartan's own pedigree was unknown, and all we know of Splinter II is that she was by Comus ex Nimble. The mating of Tartan and Splinter II produced a bitch named Worry, the dam of four champions and the grand-dam of two others.

The first Standard description of the breed appeared in Vero Shaw's *Illustrated Book of the Dog*, and was drawn up by Mr. J. B. Morrison and Mr. Thomson Gray, of Dundee (author of *Dogs of Scotland*). In the light of subsequent development of the breed it is well worth serious study:

General Appearance – is that of a thick-set, compact, short-coated terrier, standing about 9½ inches high, with body long in comparison, and averaging 16 lb. or 17 lb. weight for dogs, and 2 lb. less for bitches. Ears and tail uncut. Although in reality no higher at shoulder than the Skye or Dandie Dinmont, it has a leggier appearance from the fact that the coat is much shorter than in those two varieties. The head is carried pretty high, showing an intelligent cheery face.

Temperament – an incessant restlessness and perpetual motion, accompanied by an eager look, asking plainly for the word of command; a muscular form, fitting him for the most arduous work; and sagacity, intelligence, and courage to make the most of the situation, qualify the Scottish Terrier for the role of 'friend of the family', or 'companion in arms', in a sense unsurpassed by any other dog, large or small.

Head – is longish and bold, and is full between the eyes. It is free from long, soft, or woolly hair and is smaller in the bitch than in the dog.

Muzzle – is a most important point, and should be long and powerful, tapering slightly to the nose, which should be well formed, well spread over the muzzle, and black in colour. There must be no approach to snipeyness. The teeth should be perfectly level in front, neither being under nor overshot, fitting well together.

Eyes – are small, well sunk in the head, dark hazel, bright and expressive, with heavy eyebrows.

Ears – are very small and free from long hair, feather, or fringe; in fact, as a rule, rather bare of hair and never cut.

Neck – is short, thick, and very muscular, well set between the shoulders and showing great power.

Chest and Body – the body gives an impression of great strength, being little else than a combination of bone and muscle. The chest is broad and deep, the ribs flat – a wonderful provision of nature, indispensable to dogs often compelled to force their way through burrows and dunes on their sides. The back broad, the loin thick and very strong. This is a feature calling for special attention, as a dog in any degree weak in hindquarters lacks one of the main features of this breed and should on no account be used as a stud dog. The body is covered with a dense, hard, wet-resisting coat about two inches long.

Legs – the forelegs are short and straight with immense bone for a dog of this size. Elbows well in and not outside, the forearm particularly muscular. The hind legs are also strong, the thighs being well-developed and thick, the hocks well bent.

Feet – are small and firmly padded to resist the stony ground; nails strong, generally black. Although free from feathering, the legs and feet are well covered with hair to the very toes.

Tail – should not exceed seven or eight inches, covered with the same quality and length of hair as the body, and is carried with a slight bend, never docked.

Colour – various shades of grey, or grizzle, and brindle, the most desirable colour being red brindle with black muzzle and ear-tips.

This description, with its emphasis on that which is practical and useful, provides much food for thought. From it we can appreciate the dangers to which any breed is subject which has the show-ring as its sole criterion of merit. Every breed of dog had an original purpose for which it was bred, and the need for breeders and judges to keep this original purpose ever in mind cannot be overstressed. The Diehard is first and foremost a game, hardy, working breed, and his construction as outlined in the foregoing standard should give indication of his suitability to perform his work. The modern breeder may protest that seldom now does the modern terrier have any opportunity to prove his courage and intelligence at work, but that is no reason why his essential breed characteristics, which make him unique among dogs, should not be preserved. The more important clauses in this old standard – 'muscular form', 'teeth level', 'eyes well sunk in the head', 'great strength', 'forelegs short and straight' and 'thighs well developed and thick' – all these are qualities as much sought after today as they were seventy years ago. The general outline, as also the weight of the dog, has changed with the years, heads being longer, backs shorter, tails higher placed, bone heavier, to say nothing of the trend of fashion necessitating skilful trimming for show. But fundamentally the unique characteristics of our stout-hearted, harsh-coated popular little dog remain much unaltered.

The first show champion was a bitch named Syringa. Of unknown pedigree herself, she yet proved the foundation of one of the most successful families in the breed, a family rich in champions and still very much to the fore. (Family 6.)*

Splinter II was never a champion, but she founded a family that has since proved the largest and most prepotent in the breed. (Family 1.) She was one of the only three decent-looking terriers out of a batch of sixty sent to England by one Gordon Murray, to the order of Sir Poynton Piggott, from whom she was bought by Mr. H. J. Ludlow of Bromsgrove. To Mr. Ludlow most of the credit is due for popularizing the Scot south of the Border, and his kennel was the first of real importance in England. Of the first twenty champions recorded in the breed, he bred eight, between the years 1886 and 1894.

In 1883 he helped to found the Scottish Terrier Club of England, and was appointed its first secretary, a position he held for twenty years. He continued breedings Scots right on till the year of his death, 1908.

Type was very mixed in the early show days, even among those fortunate enough to attain the title of champion. And this title was almost as difficult to win then as it is now, but for a different reason. Usually there was only one K.C. Challenge Certificate offered, for the best of breed. It would seem that for quite a while bitches were of better quality than dogs; for in the

*This and subsequent similar notes refers to the classified Families as recorded in *Scottish Terrier Pedigrees* published 1934.

first twenty years of show competition seventeen of the champions were bitches against only eleven dogs.

Strange as it may seem, the breed has only one male line of descent throughout, right from its earliest recorded days to the present time. Mr. Ludlow owned a dog called Bonaccord, which when bred with Splinter II produced Rambler, a dog subsequently much used at stud. Rambler's mating to Worry produced three champions, one of which was Ch. Dundee, bred by Captain Mackie and born in 1882. Three years later, Dundee mated to Bitters (another from the Bonaccord–Splinter II mating) produced Ch. Lorna Doone. She in due course was put back to her grandsire Rambler, and thus gave us Ch. Alister, bred by Mr. Ludlow and born in 1885. Alister was therefore not only half-brother but also grandson of Dundee. And since these two dogs formed the first real pillars of the breed, and every living pure-bred Scot owes its male descent to one or other of them, it is of interest to study their 3-generation pedigrees:

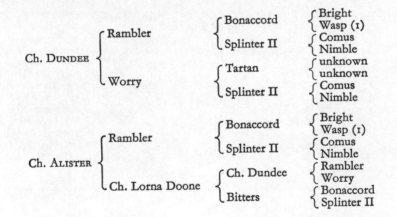

Dundee was a brindle dog, described as heavy in bone and big in ear. He was reputed to weigh 24 lb. At the Kennel Club show of 1885, a reporter stated his 'coat was so hard it might have been borrowed from a hedgehog'. He afterwards became the property of Mr. W. W. Spelman, who used the prefix Bradeston, consequently is sometimes alluded to as Ch. Bradeston Dundee.

Alister was one of the first black winners of any importance. Readers who have persevered thus far will have realized that the original colour of the breed was a light one. They were variously described as sandy, light-brindle, red-brindle, rusty-grey, grizzle, fawn, etc., and in the first standard compiled no mention whatever is made of black among the accepted colours.

It has been said that in type these two half-brothers Dundee and Alister differed somewhat, and that this contrasting type was discernible in their descendants for many long generations afterwards. Dundee sired but one champion, and that a bitch, the dam of Alister. But perhaps his most impressive contribution to posterity was through his son Highland Chief, because Chief in his turn sired Ch. Rascal. Rascal was born in 1889 and bred by Mr. J. N. Reynard, of Cambuslang, a breeder who for forty years or more devoted himself heart and soul to Scottish Terriers and their best interests. He bred many winners including three champions. In view of the fact that from Ch. Rascal this male line led on to a family tree of such consequence, it is worth noting the wealth of inbreeding behind him. Here is his pedigree:

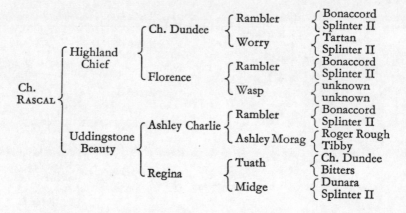

Rascal took after his paternal grandsire in being a biggish dog. He was said to grow at times a dense full coat which, added to his heavy bone, made him look even bigger than the 25 lb. he weighed. His head was clean-skulled but of more square formation than were the dogs descended in tail male from Alister. His eyes were small, his ears neat. In character he was a bold dog without shyness, a fact worth recording since it was in many of his progeny that shyness appeared in the breed. Mr. W. L. McCandlish, the greatest authority of all time on the Scottish

Terrier, wrote a monograph on the breed in 1909, and appears to attribute this tendency to shyness to a want of mental balance which went with a faulty head shape. Instead of the flat and moderately wide skull these shy terriers possessed long narrow heads, entirely without stop, the muzzle being Roman-nosed and the skull falling away towards the occiput.

Rascal sired two champion sons in Ch. Villain and Ch. Revival, but, as has happened so repeatedly in the history of our breed, it was through a non-champion son that his male line was carried on. Two generations on, and again the result of further inbreeding, the impressive sire Seafield was bred, by Mr. Andrew Kinnear of Edinburgh. He was by a dog carrying the everyday name of Jack, whose sire and dam were both by Rascal, and out of St. Clair Betsy, whose sire was Rascal and whose dam was by Rascal's sire Highland Chief.

Inbreeding was much practised in those early days. Whether by design or due to a shortage of other good material, or whether the terriers so bred proved later to be the most prepotent so that their names lived on to make history, we can only guess. However it was, undoubtedly a breed type became fixed for all time by such close concentration of the same blood.

From Seafield, mated to his half-sister, Mr. Kinnear bred Seafield Rascal, a dog entitled to be described as one of the greatest sires of the breed. Born in 1898, he died at the age of ten years, leaving a wonderful record of champions and champion-producing stock behind him. He sired six British champions, and formed the important link which kept the Dundee line in as flourishing a state as its rival, the Alister line. It is recorded that Seafield Rascal showed none of the shyness and want of *savoir faire* of which some of his progenitors had been guilty. He was essentially a masculine dog. His best son was unquestionably Ch. Heworth Rascal, bred in 1899 by Mr. Kinnear. He took his prefix from Mrs. Hannay's kennel at Heworth Hall near New-castle-on-Tyne. Mrs. Hannay was the first woman breeder and exhibitor of any note among Scottish Terriers.

Again it was through a non-champion son of Seafield Rascal's that this line was perpetuated. In his grandson Laindon Lockhart was found another influential sire. Lockhart's sire and dam were both by Seafield Rascal. He was owned by Mr. H. R. B. Tweed, of Billericay, Essex, who from about 1900 onwards till he made his last champion in 1923, did a great deal for the breed, while terriers of his Laindon prefix continually troubled the best at all the championship shows. He was for many years secretary of the South of England Scottish Terrier Club, a society which later became amalgamated with the Scottish Terrier Club (England).

Laindon Lockhart's two chief sons were Laindon Laddie and Laindon Lore. Lore, a low-to-ground dark grey brindle of Family I descent (tail female from Splinter II), left more numerous sons of note; but to Laddie fell the distinction of carrying on the Dundee male line for a further eight generations. One of the highlights of this section of the line was Mr. A. G. Cowley's first champion, Albourne Beetle, for continuing on in male descent from this dog came a truly imposing succession of Albourne-bred champions. From Laindon Lore, no less than twenty-seven champions trace their tail-male descent, but it is a regrettable fact that no male champion representative of Dundee's line have appeared since Ch. Spofford Dauntless Laddie, born in 1933. Forty or so years later it seems extremely doubtful whether any dog in direct male descent from Dundee exists in this country. Many of the best were exported, and our loss proved America's gain.

To revert to the Alister line. The most prominent sire between the years 1894 and 1900 was Heather Prince, a dog descended in tail male from Alister, whose dam was also by Alister. As we saw in the case of Seafield, the sire was mated to a sister of his dam; in the case of Heather Prince the sire was mated to a sister of his father. In other words, both Seafield and Heather Prince were results of mating with what, in human relationships we should designate as aunts. Heather Prince's sire was Prince Alexander, described as a corky short-backed dog, likewise short in head, and very much out at shoulder. His worst fault was his eyes, large and round and not sunk enough. Heather Prince was a bigger dog than his sire, and inherited his shoulders, but was a lot better in head and eye. These dogs favoured what has often been called the cart-horse type – big-boned, big-ribbed, with strong quarters, rather short in head and inclined to be thick in skull.

The prefix Heather first began to figure in the prize lists about 1893, and belonged to Mr. Robert Chapman (Senior) of Glenboig. He bred eight champions, and probably the greatest show success among these was Ch. Heather Bob, one of the six champions sired by Heather Prince. About thirty years later the prefix was revived by Mr. Chapman's two sons Robert and James, who not only kept his name Heather very much at the head of affairs in this country but made it famous throughout the world, which fame was maintained for over ten years.

History repeating itself, it was not through any of Heather Prince's champion sons that this male line was continued to link up with the present day, but through Ch. Heather Bob's litter brother Heather Dirk, whose chief claim to fame lies in the fact that he sired Scotia Prince, who sired Claymore, who in turn sired Ch. Claymore Defender. This was a thick-set short-backed dark brindle dog, whose main faults were a thick skull and a full round eye. He was, however, in considerable demand at stud, and from his mating to Ch. Bonaccord Nora, a light brindle bitch of quality, with refinement of head and a good eyes, the brothers Ch. Bapton Norman and Bapton Noble were bred. Norman created something of a stir. Born in 1909 he became a champion two years later. Few people at that time had seen such a smart well-balanced little dog, with such shortness of body and straight front. Though he possessed decent breadth of chest, his body was too much on top of his legs instead of being slung between them, and he lacked bone. Despite all that, he was somewhat in advance of his times, caught the public fancy and was extensively used at stud. Many of the breed's best bitches were bred to him, but once again, though seven champions own him as sire, it was his brother Noble on whom the maintenance of the line depended. Four of Norman's champion get were bitches, and it was in top-class females that his branch of tail-male descent ultimately petered out; with such famous names as Ch. Ornsay Doris, Ch. Ornsay Lorna, Ch. Ornsay Baba, Ch. Ornsay Queen and Ch. Bellstane Lassie. American breeders benefited by the importation of Bellstane Lassie's litter brother Bellstane Laddie, who made a strong and lasting impression on the breed in the States but was lost to us in Britain.

Another tail-male descendant from Heather Prince through his son Abertay was Ems Tonic. A hard-coated iron-grey dog of desired proportions, he proved an indifferent showman, but a glimpse I recall of him in 1906, standing keenly to attention, was something to be remembered. He deserves special mention as sire of the admittedly beautiful bitch of her day, Ch. Ems Cosmetic, and of the dog Ch. Ems Morning Nip. Cosmetic, born in 1903, was out of the Family 1 bitch Ch. Seafield Beauty. Morning Nip, born in 1908, acquires lasting notoriety from the fact that he was the first wheaten-coloured champion in the breed. His harsh dense jacket was the colour of ripe corn, tipped with black. He and Bapton Norman proved contemporaries on the bench about 1911, and according to the personal idiosyncrasy of the judge on the day took turn and turn about winning certificates. Where the Ems dog scored in clean skull, better eye placement, ears and expression, with bigger bone than Norman, the latter's straight forelegs, extra short body, higher set-on of tail and assertive demeanour, won him many a victory.

Mention of the Ems and Ornsay prefixes calls for some allusion to be made to these and certain other kennels which played a big part in the evolution of the breed from about 1905 onwards. To Mr. W. L. McCandlish, it may truly be said the breed owes more than to anyone else before or since his time. Formerly of Edinburgh, he took up residence in England and assembled his famous kennel first in Bristol, later moving to Worcestershire. He had known the Scottish Terrier in its earliest days before its recognition by the Kennel Club, and could tell much about its origin. In 1903 he succeeded Mr. Ludlow as secretary of the Scottish Terrier Club (Eng.), a task he performed with inimitable tact and efficiency until 1914. For many years he was Chairman of the Kennel Club. Few people have ever devoted so much time, care and thought over a long period for the welfare of a breed of dog as did Mr. McCandlish for the Scottish Terrier. He wrote with authority and charm, and his monograph on the breed, together with innumerable articles published, did much to foster its interests and increase its popularity. He founded his kennel upon three good bitches, all of which became champions. These were Seafield Beauty, bred by Mr. Andrew Kinnear; Ems Enya, bred by Mr. Fuller; and Ems Music, bred by the first Mr. Robert Chapman. Seafield Beauty started the famous sequence of four champion bitches in direct female descent, for her daughter Cosmetic bred Ch. Ems Vanity, and Vanity produced Ch. Ems Mode. In all, there were eight Ems-bred champions, figuring from 1905 until the First World War halted further breeding operations. The same bitch blood, however, built on such sure

Ch. Reanda Ringold

Ch. Brio Jezebel

Ch. Dundee

Ch. Ems Cosmetic
From the painting by Arthur Wardle

Ch. Light o' the Morning   George of St. Kilts

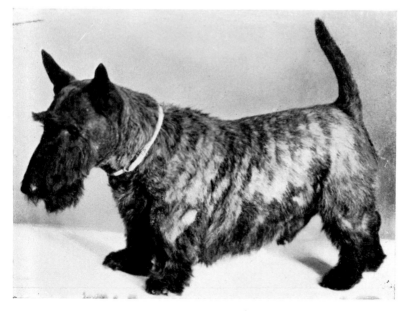

Marksman of Docken

Broxton Beau

Walsing Wizard

foundation, was not lost to the breed, since through another daughter of Cosmetic, Ems Quaintry, this section of Family 1 was supremely successful for another seven generations in the hands of Mr. A. G. Cowley. It culminated finally in the production of the black dog Ch. Albourne Barty, born in 1925, a dog to whom the term 'pillar of the breed' can most fittingly be applied.

Contemporary with the Ems era there were three kennels of equal note north of the Border, and no history of the breed can be complete without paying tribute to Mr. John Campbell of North Berwick, with his prefix of Ornsay; to Mr. George Davidson of Hawick (at this time secretary of the Scottish Terrier Club of Scotland), with his Merlewoods; and to Mr. Walter Flett of Eyemouth, who brought out winners of the Bannockburn prefix consistently from about 1905 till his death at the age of eighty in the year 1934. Scotland had ever been strongly represented by both breeders and exhibitors right on till about 1937, but since that year far too few winning Diehards have emanated from the land of their forefathers.

Three generations down from Bapton Noble in tail male, a Scottish-bred dog was bought by Mr. Tweed in the south from the well-known Abertay kennel of Mr. B. McMillan. Named Laindon Luminary and born in 1915, he became a champion five years later and proved the connecting link to carry on this male line to modern times. He was a long-headed heavily built dog, very low to ground, and was said to lack freedom of action. He sired seven champions, four of which were from Abertay-bred bitches. The litter containing Ch. Laindon Lumen and Albourne Joe (by Luminary ex Ch. Laindon Lightsome) is the one affecting the breed's history, for again it was the lesser known of the two brothers, Joe, who kept things going. The mating of Albourne Joe to Ch. Albourne Dinkie, a black bitch of advanced type linebred to Laindon Lockhart, resulted in the distinguished black dog Ch. Albourne Adair. Born in 1920, this dog may be described as one of the forerunners of an improved type as regards a pleasing combination of substance with quality.

No one taking an interest in Scottish Terriers at the shows from about 1909 onwards could fail to be impressed by the frequent recurrence of the name Albourne in the news and the prize lists. To Mr. A. G. Cowley, who owned this prefix, belongs the distinction of making a record number of champions in the

B

breed. In all, he made forty-three, and the total of British champions actually bred by him is recorded as twenty-two. Small wonder he was alluded to as the 'Albourne wizard' and deserved the title. Not only in his production of a continuous procession of winners and champions was his wizardry apparent, but in his personal association with dogs and indeed animals of all kinds. His innate gift for handling, controlling, and gaining the confidence of every type of animal is almost uncanny. All dogs take to him instinctively. Horses, dogs, and countless varieties of birds, found unapproachable or difficult to manage by most people, prove as malleable clay in the hands of Mr. Cowley. He himself disclaims all credit for his unique abilities, acknowledging them as a gift of God. Probably only once in a century is such a being born. He owned his first Scottish Terrier bitch in 1899, and the Albourne era of show-bench winners covered the period from 1909 to 1934. He also has the pen of a ready writer, and innumerable beginners in the breed owe much of their initial success to his advice.

In 1919 Mr. John Campbell bred Ch. Ornsay Brave, a dog of importance from an historical standpoint because of his bearing upon subsequent developments. He was by a grandson of Ch. Bapton Norman out of Ch. Bellstane Lassie. Lassie was by Misty Morning, a thick-set hard-coated dog which I bred in 1914, by Norman out of Ch. Light o' the Morning. The last-named was one of the 1916 batch of champions, and combined the blood of Laindon Lockhart and Ch. Ems Morning Nip. Brave proved particularly prepotent as a sire of bitches, and figured no less than eight times as the sire of dams of champions, besides having one champion daughter.

In 1925 Ch. Albourne Barty first saw the light of day. His pedigree is here set out in table opposite.

Barty was a clear instance and living embodiment of the 'Albourne wizard's' flair for breeding. Two points of importance emerge from this pedigree; one being the in-breeding to one male line throughout, and the other the intensification of the same bitch blood in both parents, for both Albourne Finesse and Albourne Huffy were of Family 1 and tail female from Ch. Ems Cosmetic. Barty was a veritable *multum in parvo*, excelling in body bone, substance and quarters. His skull was a trifle thick and his eye, though very dark, somewhat full, but he proved quite the dog of the moment both on the bench and at stud, and sired eight champions.

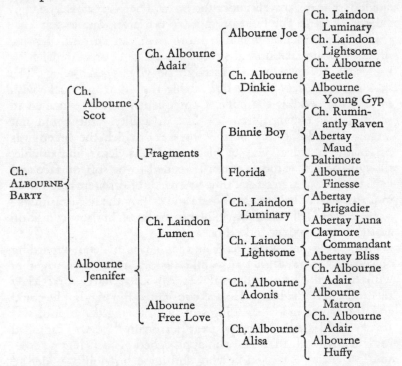

Two years after Barty there appeared on the scene a black dog of a stamp hitherto unimagined. First known by the name of Snookers Double, he was quickly snapped up by Mr. Cowley, who claimed him at a show for his catalogued price of £100. At another £100 profit he very soon passed into the hands of Mr. Robert Chapman, who was at that time ever a ready buyer of all the best available. Thereafter this sensational dog was known as Heather Necessity. He was of the same male line as Barty, being by a grandson of Ch. Albourne Adair, and his dam was by Ch. Ornsay Brave. That this dog represented a definite advance towards a type breeders were seeking seemed to be generally conceded. His critics maintained that such exaggerated length of head allied to such a short thick body verged upon the grotesque. His tail was absurdly out of proportion, a wee rudder like an inverted carrot and carried always stiffly erect, even when the dog was sitting. He had a head of excessive length for those days, but of good shape; adorned by neat little ears well placed, and small dark eyes set well under the brow. His neck would be considered short in the light of modern criticism, but was at least strong and muscular which is more than can be said of some present-day attenuations. His chest was the right breadth, with his body well swung between his straight heavily boned forelegs. The quarters were very strong but a trifle tied in at the hock, with insufficient bend at the stifle. Consequently what he gained in substance and compactness he lost in agility. One could not picture him doing any of the work for which the breed was originally intended. His jet black coat was dense and double, though somewhat too profuse. It tended to be soft on face and legs, but he had arrived at a time when exhibitors were cultivating more growth of hair on these parts and calling them 'furnishings', so he lent himself admirably to being put down in show condition all the year round, as indeed he was.

No apology is made for going rather into detail regarding Necessity, for he was a rarity and a history maker, and together with his senior and stud rival Ch. Albourne Barty, practically revolutionized the breed. He was considered too big, but he could and did, look a model standing still, and his ring demeanour was always faultless. Definitely a great personality, he was dignified yet friendly to all admirers who approached his bench at a show, and in the ring his regal bearing and imperturbability under all circumstances did much to convince the majority that not only was his type a new one but a desirable one. Many fantastic offers were made for him, but Mr. Chapman would never part. Ch. Heather Necessity created a record – subsequently broken by one of his grandsons – in the number of Challenge Certificates he won, and more times than any Scot before he went best in show all breeds. At stud he naturally commanded much patronage, and most of the breed's best matrons must have visited him. About fifteen years later one seldom read the pedigree of any pure-bred Scots without finding the name Heather Necessity figuring in it somewhere. Many of the eyes and coats of his stock were inferior to his own, but one strong and most desirable attribute he transmitted was his good temperament and his confidence. As sire of British champions he outdid Barty by accounting for eighteen – ten dogs and eight bitches; but it is worth noting that many of his best sons and daughters were from either daughters or grand-daughters of Barty.

From both Barty and Necessity this now prevailing male line increased to enormous proportions. Barty, when mated to one of the greatest producing matrons of all time – Albourne Annie Laurie – sired in one litter the Albournes, Brigand, Reveller, and Braw Lass; all three champions by the year 1929. Many considered Ch. Albourne Reveller one of the most perfect Scots yet seen. He combined quality of head with his sire's substance and body outline, inherited his dam's pleasing red-brindle colour, and was a fine free mover. He joined the Heather stud, and unfortunately did not live to a ripe old age. However, it was through him this Barty line was carried on. Mated to the dam of Ch. Heather Necessity he sired Ch. Heather Reveller, who was exported to America where he became a great stud force. Mated to a Family 1 bitch (by accident, so history relates) the resulting son was given the descriptive name of Albourne Binge Result. This little dog's comic name lived on, because from his half-sister (by Reveller) he figures as the sire of one of the greatest show dogs the breed has ever possessed. This was the black Ch. Albourne Admiration, truly well named. As his pedigree is worthy of some study, showing as it does line-breeding to so many of the best of Albourne Champions, it is set out (in the table on p. 38) to the fourth generation.

A point of interest is that eight of the sixteen great-great-grand-parents all trace in tail male back to Ch. Laindon Luminary.

Admiration was whelped in November 1930, and won his three qualifying certificates at the final three championship shows of 1931. That he was still winning certificates in 1938, and appropriated twenty-seven in all, was sufficient proof of his lasting qualities. Not for him was the midde-aged coarsening of skull that happens to many good young terriers. Nor did his perfect mouth alter. He was as good a terrier at eight years old as he had ever been. His eyes, his beautifully shaped head, the expressiveness of his perfectly placed ears and tail, his harsh flat-lying jacket, and above all his grand freedom of movement, were things always noted with approval in his Press reports throughout his career.

After making him a champion Mr. Cowley sold Admiration to

a Captain de Mowbray, who placed the dog at stud at the then excessive fee of ten guineas. Somewhat inadvisedly as later developments proved, for he was contemporary with so many of the equally famous Heather sires, regularly available to breeders at never more than a five-guinea fee. Scottish Terriers have not in the main been a hobby of the opulent, so comparatively few breeders availed themselves of the luxury of using Admiration.

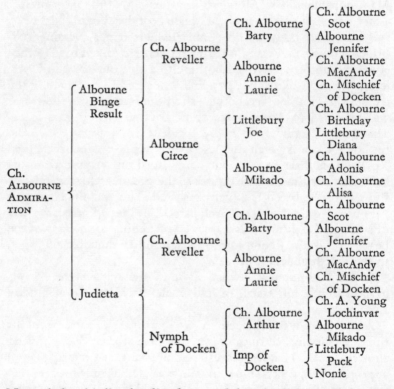

Nevertheless his line has lived on, and dogs in direct male descent from him can still be found in a few prominent kennels of today. One of his sons, Albourne Samson, begat Ch. Albourne Black Magic and the impressive sire Ch. Malgen Juggernaut. So far, eleven British champions can trace their tail-male descent from Juggernaut. Five of these were sired by Mr. R. J. Gadsden's prepotent dog Desert Emperor, a grandson of Juggernaut; while his son Walsing War Parade accounted for Ch. Walsing Winning Trick, bred by Mr. W. M. Singleton in 1946 and sold to America where his show and stud career continued to be one long series of successes.

During what might be called the reign of Ch. Heather Necessity, the years 1930 to 1936 were some of the most healthy in the breed's history. Interest was widespread, many new breeders had achieved some success, many new exhibitors had ventured forth. Show competition was never keener, and Kennel Club breed registrations soared year by year from 2,281 in 1930 to 4,497 in 1935. In 1937 these were still maintaining an average monthly total of over 300. Within this period such champions as Heather Essential, Heather Fashion Hint, Heather Ambition, Sandheys Silvertip, Crich Certainty, and Albourne Royalist qualified. All these were Necessity's sons. In addition there was Ch. Albourne Admiration qualifying in 1931, and his one and only champion son, the light grey Ch. Albourne Sandman, made up in 1934. Dr. Conrad Bremer had by that time started his wonderful sequence of champion bitches in tail female, beginning with Ch. Ortley Elegance in 1931, followed on quickly by her two daughters Ch. Ortley Carmen and Ch. Ortley Patience, both by Ch. Heather Fashion Hint.

In a breed as old as the Scottish Terrier it is obviously impossible in one chapter to touch upon all the titled dogs, or on all the important kennels, but I have tried to emphasize the importance of the new more remarkable sires which have by their prepotency left an impression and played a part in the breed's evolution.

In this category of remarkable sires, unquestionably Ch. Heather Necessity ranks high, and with his advent a new era started. People became very 'Necessity-minded'. As has already been noted the dog was extensively used at stud. It may be argued that almost any vigorous pure-bred dog, given the chances Necessity had, would have put up just as great a record. On the other hand, it is quite often found that a dog with certain features strongly exaggerated can prove a more prepotent sire than a well-balanced proportionate male of the same breed. And compared with his predecessors he undoubtedly represented exaggerations. His pedigree showed no line-breeding whatever, and looking back over the forty years which have elapsed since his day, one is forced to the conclusion that his far-reaching influence must be attributed in part to the fact that he had all the best bitches in the breed sent to him, and in part to his own dominating personality.

Of his ten champion sons, the five putting up the best show records were Heather Ambition, Heather Fashion Hint, Crich Certainty, Heather Essential, and Sandheys Silvertip. The dam of Ambition and of Essential was Ch. Albourne Romance, a daughter of Barty and strongly inbred to Family 1 and to Ch. Albourne Adair, Necessity's paternal great grandsire. Crich Certainty's dam was of the same bitch blood as the sire of Necessity's dam. Silvertip was out of that exceptional producer of champions, Albourne Annie Laurie, again of Family 1 descent. Fashion Hint was the only one of these five whose pedigree shows no line-breeding, being out of a totally unrelated bitch. Of Necessity's eight champion daughters, pride of place undoubtedly goes to Ortley Elegance and Walsing Whisper for the parts they subsequently played in building up notable families. The great ladies of the breed will be reviewed in the next chapter, but meantime suffice to say the dams of both Elegance and Whisper contributed more of the blood of Necessity's dam's sire, Ch. Ornsay Brave.

The male line of descent from Heather Necessity has been perpetuated through three main channels, all of which are rich in modern representatives. Heather Fashion Hint, bred in Scotland by Mr. J. Donald in the year 1929, was almost a replica of his illustrious sire, though a better size. He sired thirteen champions, six dogs and seven bitches, the most notable among them being the record-breaking showman, Ch. Heather Realisation, of whom more anon.

Heather Ambition, also bred in Scotland by Mr. and Mrs. Robb, in 1931, was another all-black dog of Necessity type, who sired seven champions. Three of these were of Ortley breeding, and two other Ortley-bred dogs in Ortley Endeavour and Ortley Observer, carried the line on to modern times. More or less recent representatives are the champions Heyday Hermes, Gillsie Wrockwardine Sirius, Ortley Joe, and Niddbank His Nibs.

The third son of Necessity to leave an impression on the male line was a brindle dog bred by Miss D. I. Thorpe, named Firebrand of Ralc. His chief claim to importance lies in the fact that be became gransdire of Ch. Glencannie Red Robin. This aptly named dog (A bright red brindle in colour) was bred by Mrs.

W. D. Madden in 1935 and attained his title three years later. His pedigree was interesting, for his sire was by a son of Heather Necessity out of a daughter of Fashion Hint and Ch. Albourne Red Mary; while his dam was by Ch. Crich Certainty out of the same Red Mary. It will thus be seen that Red Robin supplied a concentration of the blood of Necessity and Red Mary, the latter a beautiful bitch by Ch. Albourne Reveller and of Family 1 descent from both her parents.

Ch. Glencannie Red Robin was a grandly made dog, combining substance with quality and possessed of a lovely outline. He was somewhat temperamental, not too pleasant towards strangers, and a little variable in his ring demeanour. But none of these characteristics seem to have been transmitted to his more important descendants. He was prepotent for light colours, siring the light red brindle Ch. Brantvale Boilin' O'er who in turn sired the light grey Cr. Reimill Realist; while through his son Lambley Sandboy have come the celebrated Medwal wheatens.

To return to the most celebrated son of Ch. Heather Fashion Hint – Ch. Heather Realisation. A dark grey thick-set, low-built dog with an exceptionally hard coat and the long head of his antecedents, he was bred by Mr. Robert Chapman and born in January 1934. He came out first as an eight-months' puppy at the annual show of the S.T.C. England, where he won his first Certificate under Colonel H. R. Phipps. His second was acquired the same month at the Scottish Kennel Club show, where Mr. Cowley who was the judge that day wrote of him: 'Heather Realisation was looking possibly better than he did at the specialty show. Admitted on all sides to be an outstanding puppy, yet some thought one so young was a bit lucky to beat Ch. Albourne Admiration for the Certificate, as he did, since Admiration also was looking better than he has ever looked and is the better mover. Realisation has a shade more bone, and equal length of head of very nice type, and a topping coat.' Under a month later at just ten months old, Realisation won his third and qualifying Certificate under Major W. G. Johnson at the Kennel Club show. From then on, till the end of 1937, it was a case of 'Box and Cox' between Admiration and Realisation, though the latter had the best of it. As instance of his supremacy, of the twenty-six dog Challenge Certificates offered in the year 1936, he appropriated seventeen. In all he won forty-three, a record in the breed as yet unparalleled. He also broke all records in our breed for Best in Show awards, all breeds, for he had this honour twenty-two times. His last appearance was at Birmingham show in November 1937, where he caught a chill which turned to gastritis, to which he succumbed nine days later. A tragedy for his breeder-owner to lose this outstanding dog so young, and a distinct loss to the breed in general for he stood for several important attributes, notably his bone, substance, coat-texture, great head, and dominating personality. He has been fittingly described as a 'Pocket Hercules', and was built on similar lines to his grandsire Necessity, though not so big, and with an even longer head; also an equally disproportionate tail. He had his slight faults – what dog has not? – for his eyes were neither very dark nor deeply sunk enough, and his hind action left something to be desired.

In his all too short life, Realisation sired four champion bitches and two noted dogs. Three of his champion daughters were from bitches by Necessity, and the fourth from his halfsister, a bitch by Fashion Hint. His two noted sons were the litter brothers bred by Mr. Singleton from his Ch. Walsing Wellborn. One became Ch. Walsing Warrant and was exported before leaving much stock of note. The other was originally registered as Walsing Wonder, but on changing hands at what was rumoured to be a record price to the kennels of Mr. Chapman, his name became Heather Benefactor. Complete change of both name and prefix was then still allowed by the Kennel Club, a practice much to be deplored and productive of confusion for pedigree students; luckily it has since been abandoned, and breeders who possess a prefix now receive proper credit for breeding a good one, which is their due.

Benefactor won two Challenge Certificates while still a puppy at the end of the year 1938, but unfortunately did not live to qualify for the title he undoubtedly would have gained. He possessed all the physical virtues of his illustrious parents, and considering the enormous and ever-increasing influence of his blood upon the breed, his interesting pedigree, showing linebreeding to much of the breed's best material, is here given in the table opposite.

Certain points in this pedigree should be noted. Realisation was line-bred to the blood of Necessity and the great Annie Laurie, for among the four grandparents of his dam Gaisgill Sylvia,

Marksman of Docken and Albourne Annie Laurie were litter brother and sister; Sylvia figures again behind Juggernaut; while Wellborn brings to bear a concentration of the Barty male line, plus another dash of Necessity, while her bitch blood was the same in both halves of her pedigree (Family 2) since Malgen Starshine was full sister to Ch. Walsing Whisper.

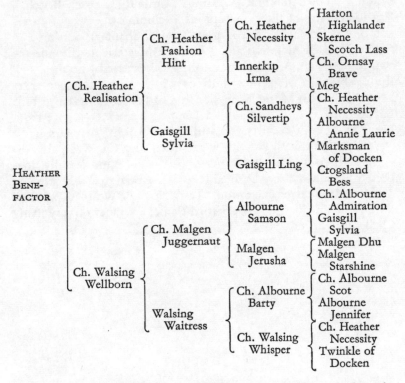

Among the last batch of champions to qualify just before the Second World War was Mr. Singleton's Ch. Walsing Woven, a bitch again inbred to Family 2, for both her grand-dams were of identical breeding, by Ch. Albourne Barty ex-Ch. Walsing Whisper. It was certainly an eventful date in the breed's history when this bitch was mated to Benefactor. The result of this intensive inbreeding was Walsing Wizard, and when the impressive number of illustrious modern winners which derive their male descent from Wizard are listed readers can see for themselves how wide has been this dog's influence, and how much is owed to

Mr. Singleton's skill as a breeder. Wizard sired one champion, the bitch Wyrebury Witching (who may be said to have started Mr. William Berry off on his successful career in the breed); while the dogs descended from him in tail male include Westpark Masterpiece (sire of seven champions, including Westpark Rio Grande and Westpark Masterman); the champion brothers Walsing Winstaino and Walsing Lomond Lancer; Rosehall Enchanter (sire of three champions, including the two of Rosehall prefix, Edward and Toryglen Tam o' Shanter); Setting Sun (sire of two champions); and Westpark Masterman (also sire of two champions). And so it goes on, for these are by no means all the celebrated male representatives which have in recent years kept this branch of the Necessity line to the fore, so that it bids fair to equal, if not excel, the other two branches – those from Heather Ambition and Glencannie Red Robin. Before leaving the tail-male topic, it should be recorded that Ch. Westpark Rio Grande, bred by Mr. A. H. James in 1948 and incidentally line-bred to Family 2 on both sides of his pedigree, has already accounted for eleven champions. These, include Westpark Romeo, the sire of Ch. Westpark Derriford Baffie, a winner of very many Challenge Certificates.

3

Families

To Mrs. C. J. Davies, resident for long years in Sussex, should go the credit for first attempting to classify Scottish Terrier pedigrees by what is known as the Bruce Lowe Figure System. This was originally propounded to apply to racehorses, and at the time Mrs. Davies wrote her book on the Scottish Terrier (published approximately 1905 or 1906) in which she gave the first attempts at this type of classification, she wrote: 'The results are hardly so marked, perhaps, in an animal which has been bred for so short a number of years as the subject of this book, as they are in racehorses which have been scientifically bred for more than 100 years; yet one cannot fail to be struck by the remarkable and peculiar results arrived at by sifting out the pedigrees of even this comparatively modern breed.'

This 'comparatively modern breed' as it was when her book appeared, has now been bred for exhibition for nearly a century, and the results derived from a study of the figure system are not only just as remarkable but far more significant today. Mrs. Davies made no attempt to classify male lines, but she did the early spade-work of compiling genealogical tables of the various Families, and many of her distinguishing numbers by which she labelled them were adhered to in subsequent works.

Mr. McCandlish had kept extensive pedigree records, as also had Mr. Robert Hussey of Chicago. Ultimately all their accumulated data came into my hands for completion, with the result that in 1934 a complete record of the pedigrees of all champions in the breed was published under the title of *Scottish Terrier Pedigrees*, and appears to have been universally accepted by breeders who give any thought to genetics, as an authentic application of the Bruce Lowe system to Scottish Terriers.

Obviously the main criterion by which we can assess the best of a breed kept primarily for show or the value of certain blood-lines, is the production of champions. Consequently the lines and families as classified and recorded are those which have produced champion progeny.

For the enlightenment of the novice it may be necessary to explain that the line of tail-male descent is represented by the top line of a displayed pedigree. In other words, it refers to the sire's sire, and his paternal grandsire and so on right back to the original male. Male descent all the way; bitches are not taken into account when referring to a male line. Conversely, the Family, or descent in tail female, is represented by the bottom line on a set-out pedigree; by the dam, and her dam, the maternal grand-dam and so on, back to the original founder bitch of the family concerned.

It may be argued there is an intermediate or middle part to any pedigree as well as the top and bottom lines, and the influence of any of the four grandparents is likely to be just as marked as any other. This is true, and where the study of pedigrees by a figure system proves both helpful and instructive is in discovering which families go to the make-up of a given dog, and whether all his or her antecedents come from recorded (champion-pro-ducing) Lines and Families, or not.

Naturally, those who have no patience with statistics need not bother their heads about the figures used for reference, but in a brief survey of the breed's most notable females such references render the subject more easily dealt with, and, I trust, somewhat clearer to the reader.

By the end of 1953 the total of British Champion Scottish Terriers made since the first bitch qualified in 1880 was 356. Forty-nine different Families (i.e. purely tail-female descent) have played their part in accounting for this imposing number, but as only sixteen of these contributed five champions or more, I propose to make allusion only to these, evidently the more prepotent.

Family 1, with Splinter II as its founder, has maintained its supremacy throughout the history of the breed, and has accounted for sixty-nine champions up to date. I will refer only to the dams which, by reason of their influence, have been the most notable. Ch. Lorna Doone, born 1884, when mated to her grandsire, provided the prepotent dog Ch. Alister. Ch. Sunray, born 1895,

mated to her close relation Heather Prince, bred Ch. Heather
Bob, and it is from Sunray and her sister Heather Mary that the
family carried right on to recent times. Ch. Seafield Beauty, born
1900, already referred to in the previous chapter, bred Ch. Ems
Cosmetic and Ems Symphony. The latter, when mated to Ch.
Bapton Norman, whelped a somewhat exceptional dog in the
dark grey Ch. Ems Troubadour, exceptional because he embodied
'the shape of things to come'. Though a thick chunk of a dog,
with big bone, he had a long and good head, ornamented by the
smallest pair of neat ears ever seen. He qualified in 1913, but
proved indifferent at stud. Cosmetic meantime bred Ch. Ems
Vanity and Ems Quaintry. Each produced champions, and the
latter provided Albourne Finesse. For Mr Cowley Albourne
Finesse did big things, for eight of the Albourne champions were
produced in direct descent from her. These were the bitches
Albourne Alisa, Albourne Anita, and Albourne Kiltie; and the
champion dogs Albourne Scot, Albourne Adonis, Albourne
MacAdair, Albourne Arthur, and the maker of history, Albourne
Barty.

In 1902, Mr. W. M. Cumming, who had an influential kennel
in those days, in Scotland, bred Bonaccord Jewel, three generations in tail female from Ch. Sunray. Jewel was a substantial
black bitch with very nice head and outlook, but what in these
days would be considered too long a body and a low-set tail.
Mated to the Family 1 dog Seafield Rascal she bred Ch. Bonaccord Peggy, a black bitch very like her dam in head but smarter
and shorter-backed. Jewel later became the property of Mr.
Tweed who put her to Laindon Lockhart and bred Laindon
Polly (dam of Ch. Laindon Lens) and a bitch called Lola. From
Lola a succession of good winners were bred, culminating ten
generations further on in Kiltane Echo, the dam of Ch. Heather
Beau Ideal. Six generations from Ch. Bonaccord Peggy came
Ch. Mischief of Docken, bred by Mr. J. Vanson and born in
1923. She represented a concentration of this famous family since
she was the result of mating a bitch to her own son. That this
close breeding had some bearing on the prepotency of her progeny
is more than likely, for she became the dam of the noteworthy
couple Marksman of Docken and Albourne Annie Laurie in one
litter, bred by Mrs. Scrase-Dickins in 1924, whose Docken prefix
was much to the fore from around that date until the Second

World War. Marksmen remained in his breeder's ownership all his life and attained a grand old age. Though he sired a few dams of champions he did not have the luck to leave any impressive sons. He was a pale silver-grey in colour, a great dog in every sense of the word, grandly proportioned throughout; maybe a trifle long-cast but with great depth of brisket, ribs carried well back, strong loin, huge bone and powerful quarters. His coat texture was not his fortune, but his greatest handicap was his size, for he was built on a very large scale. He had terrific character and a perfect temperament. His sister Annie Laurie (first registered as Melody of Docken) was a red brindle, hard-coated and the right size, and accepted in her day as one of the best yet seen, but as a show proposition she was disappointing owing to her bashful temperament. She changed hands three times. Her first handler had but little success with her. The next owner was Mr. Cowley who got sufficient response from her to win several prizes at championship shows during 1925, though she was invariably beaten by her dam. By this time her name had been changed and it was in the Albourne kennels she became the dam of her first four champion progeny. Mated to Littlebury Jerry (of Family 1 descent) she produced Ch. Albourne Lamplighter. By Ch. Albourne Barty (likewise of Family 1) she performed the astonishing feat of three champions from one litter, these being the Albournes Brigand, Reveller and Braw Lass. By 1927 Mr. Cowley had sold her to Mr. Richard Lloyd of Southport, whose prefix of Sandheys was then figuring in the news. He put her first to another Family 1 dog in Ch. Tweburn Clincher, and from this mating bred Ch. Sandheys Sentry. Two years later he mated her to Ch. Heather Necessity, the result being the very handsome low-built and great-headed dog Ch. Sandheys Silvertip. He was mainly black, with slight brindle markings on the legs and a definite silver star below his tail, hence his name. It will thus be seen Annie Laurie produced in all six champions, an astounding record for a bitch.

From Heather Mary, the sister of Ch. Sunray, came a very useful succession of bitches of the Littlebury prefix, bred by Mrs. Burrell of Cambridge. Owing to a physical infirmity this keen breeder could not handle her own exhibits, but fellow-fanciers used to lend a hand and she made three champions, all in tail female from Littlebury Nancy. These were Ch. Albourne

Birthday, Ch. Littlebury Nona and Ch. Cheer of Corse. Five generations on from Nancy appeared Ch. Albourne Red Mary, the dam of Ch. Glencannie Red Robin and grand-dam of Heather Marina who produced the dog Ch. Heather Independence. The latest Family 1 champion qualified in 1948, but without doubt a day will return when this most prolific family in the breed will increase and multiply again to its former proportions. Others that have graced it and should be mentioned are Ch. Claymore Defender, Ch. Writtle Patricia, Ch. Lovegift of Lammermuir, Ch. Jean of Corse, Ch. Ornsay Gorst, Ch. Spofford Dauntless Laddie and Ch. Gillsie Wrockwardine Sirius.

Family 2 originated with Scottish Maid and her two daughters. Both these led to branches of increasing influence, one branch containing a succession of noted Merlewood bitches, including Ch. Merlewood Hopeful and Ch. Merlewood Cleopatra, and the other leading to the famous Tattenhams. This latter prefix belonged to Mrs. E. S. Quicke, a very astute breeder and most popular judge. The basis of her breeding experiments was a smart little black bitch named Madre Tordo, which was of Clonmel blood and bred by the late Mr. Holland Buckley, whose Clonmel prefix at that time counted almost as much in Scots as it did in Airedales. Madre Tordo represented the eighth generation down from Scottish Maid, and was sired by a son of Ch. Bapton Norman, whom she greatly resembled in type. Mating her to Brockwell Jack, a son of the aforementioned Ch. Bonaccord Peggy, Mrs. Quicke bred Scricciolo, a brown brindle bitch with better bone than her dam but still somewhat on the leg. Scricciolo was then put to the low-swung heavily built Laindon Lore, which mating meant inbreeding to the male line, that of Laindon Lockhart. The result was two dogs which had immense influence, Waterford Wagtail and Lorehart. Mrs. Quicke retained Wagtail and did considerable winning with him. He was a grey brindle dog, whose head was reported upon as perfect, with good eyes, small ears and keen expression. In general conformation he was excellent, and had it not been for a slightly unlevel mouth he would no doubt have become a champion. In due course Scricciolo was mated to him, her own son, and produced Ch. Tattenham Treasure. The following year, 1919, this mating was repeated, resulting in Ch. Tattenham Treat. Both these delightful bitches qualified as champions in 1920. They embodied a happy blend of the longer head, better depth of body and lowness to ground, inherited from Laindon Lore, with the smart compactness and alert bearing of the dam's ancestry, of which, through Wagtail, they possessed a double dose. Ch. Tattenham Treasure proved the main corner-stone of Family 2. She had two important daughters, Tattenham Tulip and Tattenham Tweak. Tulip's grand-daughter produced two champion dogs in Rookery Repeater and Albourne Highlander; while Tweak supplied the breed with three champion-producing branches. One led to Ch. Wilforths Wat-a-Lass, who was exported. Another led through two bitches of the Lambley prefix and two of the Medwal prefix to Westpark Bubblin' O'er, the dam of Ch. Westpark Rio Grande, and to Medwal Miss Music, the dam of the wheaten brother and sister Ch. Medwal Wild Oats and Ch. Medwal Musidora. The third branch, recently extending in many directions and making history all the way, was through her daughter Tattenham Twink. Pause for a moment to consider the intensive inbreeding. Tweak had been produced by mating Ch. Treasure back to her sire's sire Laindon Lore. Twink was the result of mating the already close bred Tweak to Waterford Wagtail, who was not only her half-brother, since both were sired by Lore, but also her uncle and her maternal grandsire! If one takes the trouble to jot down the above details in the usual manner of displayed pedigrees it will be seen that Tattenham Twink's blood was literally nothing else but that of Laindon Lore and Scricciolo. Small wonder, perhaps, that her blood has proved so prepotent. When mated to Ch. Ornsay Brave she bred Twinkle of Dockend and Hawdonside Vixen. The latter, mated to Marksman of Docken, produced a glorious bitch in Ch. Hawdonside Melody. Twinkle of Docken was mated to Ch. Heather Necessity in 1930 and bred a large litter, of the quality of which, when very young, the breeder and others did not appear to think very highly. A red brindle bitch from this litter is reputed to have changed hands for a mere £3. She proved the foundation of Mr. Singleton's famous Scottish Terrier kennel, and became Ch. Walsing Whisper, qualifying in 1932. Family 2 has produced in all thirty-nine champions so far, and when it is realized that eighteen of these trace their female descent from Whisper, her great influence on the breed will be appreciated. These include the bitches Ch. Ripple of Rookes, Ch. Walsing Waterlily, Ch. Walsing Wellborn,

Ch. Walsing Woven, Ch. Lomond Lovely Lady, Ch. Wyrebury Witching, Ch. Glenview Gay Girl, Ch. Walsing Wild Revel, Ch. Wyrebury Witchcraft, Ch. Wyrebury Watercress, Ch. Carron Castile, and Ch. Wyrebury Woodnymph; and the dogs Ch. Walsing Warrant, Ch. Walsing Winstaino, Ch. Walsing Lomond Lancer, Ch. Wyrebury Wonder, Ch. Wyrebury Waiter, Ch. Wyrebury Welldoer, and Ch. Westpark Derriford Baffie. The fact that Ch. Malgen Juggernaut was also a Family 2 dog, grandson of Whisper's full sister, is important, for he sired Ch. Walsing Wellborn and figures frequently in the pedigrees of several other champions.

Family 3, tail female from Bannockburn Stumpie, has never been a large group but has given us twenty-three champions for all that. Some of its best bitches in the past were Ch. Glory, Ch. Heather Nellie, and Ch. Ems Mode; while two very typical terriers in Ems Bhanavar and Chandos Pearl proved respectively the dams of the dogs Ch. Heworth Bantock and Ch. Albourne Beetle. Ems Excuse, granddaughter of Bhanavar, contributed the wheaten Ch. Ems Morning Nip. Another bitch of note in this family was Ornsay Matron, for she contributed two famous daughters of grand type in Ch. Ornsay Lorna, born in 1924, and Ch. Ornsay June, in 1926; while from another of her daughters three generations of Niddbank bitches resulted, bred by Mrs. K. M. Ross. Her Niddbank Lady Mary, when mated to My Ideal of Glenview, bred Ch. Niddbank Blue Print, in 1947, and two years later to Allbright Dragoon, bred Ch. Niddbank His Nibs. Apart from these two dogs, the only moderately recent notabilities to grace Family 3 have been Ch. Glenellen Gentleman and Ch. Reimill Realist.

Family 4 originated with a bitch called Old Nell and her two daughters. It has proved a prolific family, with a strong tendency to produce a preponderance of notable males, for of the thirty-three champions tracing their female descent from Old Nell, twenty-one have been dogs. And when it is seen that among these are such eminent characters as Ch. Bapton Norman, Ch. Laindon Luminary and Ch. Lauriston Leaper before the First World War, and in quite recent years Ch. Westpark Beau Geste, Ch. Wyrebury Maigarth Martinet and Ch. Wyrebury Wrangler, it will be agreed that Family 4 is by no means a bad one to belong to. Some of its most famous bitches have been Ch. Hagar, of 1892, short-headed but good-bodied it was said; Undercliffe Rosie, who bred two champions in 1902 in one litter by Seafield Rascal, these being Ch. Bonaccord Sandy and Ch. Bonaccord Nora – the dam of Ch. Bapton Norman; Carter Jean, the dam of two champion dogs; and Lauriston Lydia, whose name figures in the tail female of twelve champions. Ch. Wyrebury Maigarth Mazurka, bred in 1948 by Mr. J. L. Deas, traces back to Laurieston Lydia in ten generations.

Family 5 is comparatively small but extremely select. From its founder, twelve generations were bred, of a steadily improving quality, until Albourne Glendalyne was produced, a fairly big substantial bitch who looked cut out for the vocation of brood matron, which she undoubtedly proved. From the branches resulting from her three daughters, twelve champions have been bred. Glendalyne herself was sired by Laindon Lockhart, and it is worth noting that each of her three impressive daughters were sired by dogs descended in tail male from Lockhart. The notabilities this family can claim include Ch. Albourne Dinkie and her famous son Ch. Albourne Adair; Ch. Albourne Romance and her two famous sons Ch. Heather Essential and Ch. Heather Ambition; while getting down to more recent times the bitch Miss Cleave bred two champions in Ch. Westpark Masterman and Ch. Westpark Mistress, the latter in her turn becoming the dam of Ch. Westpark Refreshed.

The distinction of tracing in tail female from the breed's first champion falls to Family 6. Little is known of the founder Ch. Syringa, except that she existed about 1877. Ten generations of bitches in direct female descent from her led to the production in one branch of Ladhope Lilac, the dam in 1912 of Ch. Ellwyn Adam; and in the other branch at about the same date the bitch Meadow Lass, who was the result of mating a bitch to her own sire. Meadow Lass belonged to Mr. A. Collins of Edinburgh, who bought Misty Morning from me in 1916 and the following year bred from these two a litter of far-reaching importance. These were known as the Bellstanes, one dog and three bitches, Laddie, Lassie, Beauty and Lady. Laddie, as previously mentioned, went to the U.S.; Lassie, bought by Mr. John Campbell, became a champion in his hands, and also the dam of the influential dog Ch. Ornsay Brave, and the two bitches Ch. Ornsay Queen and Ch. Ornsay Doris. Lady bred Merlewood Typist, the dam of

Ch. Merlewood Aristocrat; while Beauty produced three daughters, all of which had a role of importance, one breeding the dam of Ch. Crich Certainty, another producing a champion daughter, and the third having the signal honour of being progenitress of every one of the Ortley celebrities. Dr. Conrad Bremer, who owns the Ortley prefix, is the only breeder as yet to equal the record put up by Mr. McCandlish of breeding three champion bitches in sequence. Bellstane Beauty's grand-daughter Lutton Belle produced Ortley Violet Ray, the basic bitch behind all the Ortleys, and worth noting is the fact that Violet Ray's sire was also of Family 6, being a grandson of Bellstane Beauty. For a time Dr. Bremer used the Heather sires which were then at the zenith of their success, and his first champion was Ch. Ortley Elegance, born in 1930, by Ch. Heather Necessity out of Ortley Violet Ray. She was quickly followed by Ch. Ortley Carmen the following year, bred the same way. Ch. Ortley Patience, born in 1932, was also from Elegance but sired by Ch. Heather Fashion Hint. Yet another champion bitch from Elegance was Ch. Ortley Bridget, born in 1935 and bred the same way as Patience. But in the meantime Ch. Ortley Angela had come upon the scene, by Ch. Heather Ambition out of Ch. Ortley Carmen; also the dog Ch. Ortley Pilot, likewise by Ambition but from Ortley Donna Clara who was half-sister to Elegance. Ch. Ortley Marion, born in 1934, was bred the same way as Ch. Ortley Patience. Mention should be made at this point of Ortley Endeavour, full brother to Ch. Ortley Angela. Though not a champion, he sired four, and it was his mating to Ortley Donna Clara, thus intensifying the Family 6 blood, that produced Ch. Ortley Prima Donna in 1935. Prima Donna became the dam of Ortley Christina, dam of Ch. Ortley Monty and of Ortley Margaret, who in her turn bred two noted sons in Ch. Ortley Simon and Ch. Ortley Joe. Joe's pedigree is actually five-eighths Family 6, for he was sired by Rosehall Ambassador, who was Ortley-bred both sides. Up to the time of writing Dr. Bremer has bred fourteen champions. In addition to the Ortleys, this family, again through Violet Ray, is also responsible for Ch. Wenbury Westpark Superman, Ch. Brantvale Boilin' O'er, Ch. Westpark Sunfair, Ch. Lowthian Linda, and Ch. Sedgway Christine.

With the history of Family 7 it is comparatively easy to deal, because all its nine champions owe their female descent to one bitch named Glenluce. She was the dam of the only noted dog ever sired by Ch. Ems Troubadour, in Ch. Ruminantly Raven, and four of her daughters all led to champion-producers. Glenluce was a very oversized lady with a great long head, great long body to match, and tail likewise. But she transmitted certain virtues to her descendants, the chief of which were real harsh coats, great ribs, and a capacity for easy whelping, and in three generations any tendency to length in the wrong places was firmly bred out. Having been privileged to breed, own, or kennel several generations of this family, from Glenluce's grand-daughter Glenfannich onwards, I can vouch for their useful qualities; and two crosses of the extra short-backed Break o' Day, litter-brother to Misty Morning, gave Blackmill Baroness, the dam, in 1926, of Ch. Talavera Toddler. The family was then quiescent for a while until Ch. Sandheys Steady Lad, out of a half-sister of Baroness, qualified in 1935 at four years old. The same year the wonderful-bodied and coated bitch, Ch. Desco Desire, was bred by Mr. and Mrs. John Dewar from Ortley Endeavour and the very short-bodied great-grand-daughter of Blackmill Baroness, Desco Diana. Also in 1935, from another branch of Glenluce descent, appeared the bitch Ch. Rosehall Ideal. Twelve generations from Glenluce came Ch. Allbright Gay Model in 1945, and nine generations from Blackmill Baroness figure Ch. Viewpark Vanity Girl and Ch. Viewpark Pilot. Another adornment to this family is Ch. Silver Melody, the grey bitch qualifying in 1952 whose name was so much in the news as a Best in Show winner, all breeds.

The next group responsible for giving the breed not less than five champions is Family 10, which has Ch. Delings Warrior, Ch. Rosehall Edward, Ch. Reimill Chorus Girl, Ch. Rosehall Toryglen Tam o' Shanter and Ch. Con of Conett to its credit.

Family 12, on the other hand, is a large and ever-increasing group, and has accounted for fifteen champions up to date. Without question its most notable achievement was the production of Ch. Heather Realisation, out of Gaisgill Sylvia, a good bitch who was reputed to be too shy to show. Sylvia's dam, Gaiskill Ling, had never been shy, and she bred another good daughter in Ch. Gaisgill Monah. Sylvia also contributed another champion in Ch. Gaisgill Minnie, and directly descended from her five generations further we come to the modern representative of this family, Miss Bull's Ch. Kennelgarth Mallich. Another of its many branches proceeded through several of the Merlewood prefix to culminate in the red brindle dog Ch. Rochford Sandboy; and this same branch, by means of Ch. Heather Patience, led to several Glenview bitches, finally ending again with a dog in the shape of Ch. Gillsie Turfield Dramatic, since exported.

Family 15 can boast of the dams of four famous dogs, but has so far only produced one champion bitch, this being Ch. Laindon Lightsome, dam of Ch. Laindon Lumen. As two of the dogs were the remarkable Ch. Heather Necessity and Ch. Heather Reveller, both out of Skerne Scotch Lass, the notoriety of this family is assured for all time.

The production of champions tracing their descent from Langholm Peggy and recorded as Family 16 has been spread over a long period of years. The first was the dog Ch. Keppoch Dugald, in 1909; the second appeared seven generations and twenty years later, being the bitch Ch. Lonkley Larkspur; while yet another seventeen years elapsed before Ch. Medwal Miss Mustard qualified in 1947, and had the distinction of being only the second wheaten champion in the breed. She in her turn bred Ch. Medwal McTavish, and the same branch of the family, tail female from Medwal Mystery, has provided, qualifying in 1953, the wheaten dog Ch. Bidfield Bix.

Of no great age is the record of Family 22, for its first notable dog, Ch. Rantin Sir Ian, qualified in 1913. He was the result of mating Clockiel Cis to her uncle, and his sister Ornsay Judy produced four daughters whose descendants have produced in all five champions. Mention need only be made of two of these, since they have proved so distinguished; Ch. Heather Fashion Hint, born in 1929, was from Innerkip Irma, four generations from Ornsay Judy; and Ch. Walsing Winning Trick, born in 1946, was out of Walsing Whymper, ten generations from the same Judy.

From its founder bitch Kingarth Jenny, Family 26 extended in a very short time to many influential branches and boasts of some very great matrons. This family has so far produced fourteen champions, the earliest, Ch. Bannockburn Howdie, being bred in 1919, and the two most recent, Ch. Garleves Estrellita and Ch. Seawave Maybelle, in 1948. Probably its two greatest producers have been Craigieburn Dina, who in one litter bred both Ch. Craigieburn Bard and Ch. Albourne Capture; and Dunsappie, the dam of two champions in Ch. Heather Enchantress and Ch Rose Marie of Rookes. Ch. Walsing Watchlight, bred in 1945, and Ch. Rosehall Eldin Brenda, born 1947, also owe their descent to this family.

Family 33 is the next of importance. It has accounted for 23 champions, and its six branches all tracing from the common ancestress Heather Rose have spread widely in a comparatively short period of time, In tail female from Pearl (sometimes known as Johnston Baroness) came four prolific sections, one of its earliest productions being the bitch Ch. Misty Morn of Ralc who qualified in 1931, and whose sire Ch. Laurieston Landseer was a product of the same family. There were many notable bitches of the Rosehall prefix figuring between 1931 and 1934, all originating from Rosehall Lass (dam of Ch. Rookery Adair) who was great-grand-daughter of Pearl. Then this family made a great come-back after the Second World War, producing Ch. Desert Viscountess in 1946, Ch. Westpark Moonta Mauna, Ch. Glenrae Prince Charming and Ch. Markham Miranda in 1948, and Ch. Westpark Achievement. Ch. Black Abbess of Veena and Ch. Medwal McKye in 1949. Since then a mass of champions of the Moonta prefix have appeared, all tracing to the prepotent Moonta Mharhadhu, who was six generations after Pearl. The latest to qualify have been Ch. Granthorpe Alice in 1952, and Ch. Gregorach Mull in 1954, these through different branches from the Pearl section, but still tracing direct from Heather Rose.

Since Family 39 first made its presence felt with Ch. Brave Vixen, born in 1924 by Ch. Ornsay Brave out of Black Vixen, nothing more of note appeared for over twenty years, until Mr. A. H. Gee bred some good bitches from Hartspike Hazel, who traced back six generations in direct descent to the litter sister of Ch. Brave Vixen. Hazel mated to her half-brother produced Glenview Greta (the dam of Ch. Glenview Grace) and Glenview Glennis. Glennis when mated to Mr. Gee's well-known winner My Ideal of Glenview (a son of Ch. Brantvale Boilin' O'er and a Family 5 bitch) bred the dog Ch. Glenview Idealist and his sister Glenview Ideal Lass. The latter was put back to her own sire and bred Ch. Glenview Guardsman, who qualified in 1952. She was then mated to her own full brother Idealist, which mating produced Ch. Glenview Grand Lass, qualifying in 1953.

The next Glenview-bred champion appeared the same year in Glenview Sir Galahad, a result of very close inbreeding again, for his sire was by My Ideal out of his own daughter (a full sister to Grace), and his dam was Ideal Lass who, as stated above, was also by My Ideal.

The only other family to give the breed as many as five champions is numbered 42, which from a somewhat indifferent class of black bitches named Psyche and Phyllis, a mother and daughter I remember way back in 1917, distinct advance was made in three generations to Croindene Cabaret Girl, the dam of Ch. Albourne Black Magic and three useful daughters. Tracing from one of these came Ch. Heather Coronation; from another Ch. Notley News Girl; and from the third Ch. Heyday Hermoine, who has in her turn bred a champion dog in Ch. Heyday Hermes, who qualified in 1950.

There is another family to which a new distinguishing number has been given, it having come into prominence only in recent years. It traces back twenty-two generations in tail female and is proved to belong to one of the earlier known families. It rose to fame in the hands of Mrs. E. Meyer, who bred the famous Reanda Rosita who belongs to family 23. In the year 1909 this family was represented by only one champion, Mr. Tweed's lovely bitch Laindon Locket. But a full sister of Locket, called Gimlette and owned by Miss Gentry, carried on the female line, and through a succession of bitches, in the hands first of the Hon. Mrs. Fordham and later of Mrs. Lovett, fourteen generations further on appeared the founder bitch of Mrs. Meyer's successful Kennel, Reanda Medwal Marchioness, the grand-dam of Rosita. From the thirty British Champions Mrs. Meyer has bred or owned, nine were out of Rosita herself. Rosita has thus beaten the record previously held by the Family 1 bitch Albourne Annie Laurie, as a dam of champions.

Line-breeding to a family, or to the bitch blood, does carry weight as has been proved. So also, it may be argued, does line-breeding to the male blood. Whichever practise is followed, one must first know fully the material to which one is inbreeding, and as far as possible its potentialities. The value of a study of the female lines, or families, in a breed lies in the fact that a bitch can produce in her life a very small number of progeny in comparison to a dog. She may raise from four to ten pups per annum as against the sixty to a hundred a popular dog may sire, therefore her chance to prove her worth as a breeder is comparatively small. Consequently, where a good bitch comes from a long line of good bitches, some of which have at times produced champions, the element of uncertainty as to what she herself may breed is, to say the least of it, reduced. We are all acquainted with the sort of pedigree the bottom of line of which trails off into such names as Nell, Jean, or Kate, meaning as a rule less than nothing for 'Kate's' origin is usually unknown, but when a bitch traces to a recorded family in all her female ancestry she is the more likely to have within her the latent capacity to breed a desirable type of pup. Naturally 'the proof of the pudding is in the preeing' and no one can with certainty foretell just how much a given bitch inherits from her forbears and how many of their good qualities she can transmit until she is tried out. Occasionally a chance-bred bitch may throw some good stock, but in retaining any such stock we are not building on so sure a foundation as when we know her antecedents and their capabilities.

The records of *Scottish Terrier Pedigrees* are now kept and are being continued by Mrs E. Blower, Echo Hill, Sleights, Whitby, Yorkshire, to whom enquiries on this subject can be made.

4

The Breed Standard

THERE are now nine Specialist Clubs in Great Britain and N. Ireland, serving the interests of the Scottish Terrier, the oldest club being the Scottish Terrier Club of England which was founded in 1883. Its objects and those of its fellow-societies, are: (a) to promote the breeding of pure Scottish Terriers; (b) to adopt and publish a description of type and standard of points and to urge the adoption of this type on Breeders, Judges, Dog Show Committees, etc., as the only recognized and unvarying standard by which Scottish Terriers are to be judged; and (c) to do all in its power to protect and advance the interests of the breed by offering prizes, supporting certain shows, and taking any other steps that may be deemed advisable.

The Scottish Terrier Club of Scotland was founded in 1888, and the standards of points drawn up by both these original clubs were virtually the same, only differing slightly in point valuations, and served their purpose for about fifty years. The various points had a percentage of values attached to them, thus: Skull, 5; Muzzle, 5; Eyes, 5; Ears, 10; Neck, 5; Chest, 5; Body, 15; Legs and Feet, 10; Tail, 2½; Coat, 15; Size, 10; Colour, 2½; General Appearance, 10. In 1932 a specially selected committee was appointed to revise the standard. This consisted of five people: Mr. W. L. McCandlish, Mr. A. G. Cowley, Col. H. R. Phipps, Mr. Jack Edwards and Mrs. D. S. Caspersz. Twelve months later the wording as it now stands was agreed upon by the Scottish Terrier Club of England and later adopted by the Kennel Club as being the only Scottish Terrier Standard:

General Appearance. A Scottish Terrier is a sturdy, thick-set dog of a size to get to ground, placed on short legs, alert in carriage, and suggestive of great power and activity in small compass. The head gives the impression of being long for a dog of its size. The body is covered with a close-lying, broken, rough-textured coat, and with keen intelligent eyes and sharp prick ears the dog looks willing to go anywhere and do anything. In spite of its short legs, the construction of the dog enables it to be very agile and active. The whole movement of the dog is smooth, easy and straightforward, with free action at shoulder, stifle and hock.

Head and Skull. Without being out of proportion to the size of the dog it should be long, the length of skull enabling it to be fairly wide and yet retain a narrow appearance. The skull is nearly flat and the cheek-bones do no protrude. There is a slight, but distinct drop between skull and foreface just in front of the eye. The nose is large, and in profile the line from the nose towards the chin appears to slope backwards.

Eyes. Should be almond-shaped, dark brown, fairly wide apart and set deeply under the eyebrows.

Ears. Neat of fine texture, pointed and erect.

Mouth. Teeth large, the upper incisors closely overlapping the lower.

Neck. Muscular, of moderate length.

Forequarters. The head is carried on a muscular neck of moderate length showing quality, set into a long sloping shoulder, the brisket well in front of the forelegs, which are straight, well boned to straight pasterns. The chest is fairly broad and hung between the forelegs, which must not be out at elbows nor placed under the body.

Body. The body has well-rounded ribs, which flatten to a deep chest and are carried well back. The back is proportionately short and very muscular. In general, the top line of the body should be straight; the loin muscular and deep, thus powerfully coupling the ribs to the hindquarters.

Hindquarters. Remarkably powerful for the size of the dog. Big and wide buttocks. Thighs deep and muscular, well bent at stifle. Hocks strong and well bent and neither turned inwards nor outwards.

Feet. Of good size and well padded, toes well arched and close-knit.

Tail. Of moderate length to give a general balance to the dog, thick at the root and tapering towards the tip, is set on with an upright carriage or with a slight bend.

Coat. The dog has two coats, the undercoat short, dense and soft; the outercoat harsh, dense, and wiry; the two making a weather-resisting covering to the dog.

Colour. Black, wheaten, or brindle of any colour.

Weight and Size. The ideally made dog in hard show condition could weigh from 19 lb. to 23 lb. Height at shoulder ten to eleven inches.

In compiling this standard, the aim was to supply a word-picture of an ideal dog, and point valuations and list of faults were done away with. Anyone who aspires to success either as a breeder, exhibitor or judge would do well to peruse this standard frequently and devote serious thought to it. If considered intelligently it should conjure up a mental vision of a Scottish Terrier of the correct breed type, but since it becomes increasingly evident that a number of breeders either never refer to the Standard, or if they do, fail to grasp its full significance, it seems desirable to examine this official description in detail in order to clarify if possible the meaning not fully understood.

The first facts to lay hold of are that the Scottish Terrier is a working breed and that he is unique among breeds of dog. The original purpose for which any breed was evolved should never be lost sight of. The whole structure of the Scottish Terrier is in keeping with the work he was intended to do both above and below ground. A badly made terrier could probably do the same work, but a properly constructed one will do it better and at the same time give more pleasure by being nicer to look at. The time-worn retort that show dogs do not work is pointless, for every breed of domesticated dog had at some stage in its history a specific purpose for which it was kept and bred, and the compilers of a standard of points for any breed must perforce keep this original purpose ever uppermost in their minds. The sturdy Diehard was never intended to pull a cart, or to run races, to lounge on silken cushions, or to be a clown. That he can do all these things if trained is proof of his adaptability, but he was originally meant to go to ground after badger, otter, etc., to burrow and to kill, and at the same time be agile enough to spring from rocks and boulders in the course of searching out his quarry. Probably nowadays the toughest prey he is ever called upon to kill is a rat, and as a killer he has few compeers. The essential thing to bear in mind is that the dog's appearance should convey his *ability* to do his rightful work even if he doesn't have to.

That the whole build of the Scot is unique should be self-evident, for in what other breed does one find such power and substance in small compass, such heavily boned short legs, such a thick-set muscular body, such immense power in the loin and hindquarters, and such a large head for a dog of the size; the whole topped by erectly carried ears and tail. The nearest comparisons are his first cousins the West Highland White and the Cairn terriers, but they are not low-to-ground, nor required to be so substantial or so heavy in bone, nor is the body slung between the legs as in the Scot.

The Standard description strikes the right note at the very beginning with the words 'of a size to get to ground'. The fact that the standard weight has now a maximum of 23 lb. as against the former 21 lb. has fortunately made but little difference to actual results in the show-ring. Weight and size must not be confused. The modern dog weighs more than his forbears by reason of his greater bone and substance as he more nearly approaches the ideal of possessing 'great power and activity in small compass', but he is in the main no bigger.

As this first phrase suggests, if a dog is of the size to get to ground he must by implication be keen to do so, and the further clause about his looking 'willing to go anywhere and do anything' sets the seal on an all-round useful terrier. Be he kept for breeding only, or as the all-purpose canine companion and house-guard in town or country, as a pet or a worker, or purely as a show specimen, his bearing and appearance should at all times denote the gameness, strength, courage and common sense that are part and parcel of a Scot's make-up. Cast an eye through the whole standard and note the number of times words indicating power are included. At the start we find 'great *power* and activity in small compass'. We are told that the nose and the teeth must be *large*, both indications of a stout-hearted strong dog. The neck must be *muscular*, chest *fairly broad*, as befits a Hercules in miniature. The back is described as *very muscular*, the loin *muscular and deep* thus *powerfully* coupling the ribs to the hindquarters. And last, but by no means least, in the paragraph on hindquarters we find these must be *remarkably powerful*, the thighs *deep and muscular*, and the hocks *strong*. Everything is suggestive of strength.

Actually nothing so conveys the correct breed type as the right sort of hindquarters. The key to the correct build of a Scot lies in the bend at stifle and hock. Unless these are right everything else is likely to be wrong. The difficulty is to explain what is right to those who have never seen it, but looking at the dog from the side, the hindquarters should look almost as if he were set on a spring, and as if at any moment the spring would open out and the dog be in the air. The upper thigh should be tremendously thick from back to front and the underline of the thigh should almost curve in to the horizontal. The springing ability of a well-

HEAD

1. Correct stop and relative length of skull and foreface   2. Lack of stop

constructed Scot is often surprising; from a standing start he can be on the floor one moment and on a three-foot high table the next.

One would think the official description of Head leaves no room at all for doubt as to what is required to constitute a good head, yet to read the show reports of some judges or listen to some breeder's remarks, it is obvious that misconceptions are rife. The head should be long, without being out of proportion to the size of the dog. Of that much breeders and others have been fully aware ever since Scottish Terriers were first exhibited. But in striving after sheer length at the expense of correct shape nothing is gained, while the characteristic profile and typical expression are lost. A natural consequence in any breed of breeding for excessive length of head is the elimination of the stop. The Standard quite clearly lays down the necessity for a 'slight, but distinct drop between skull and foreface just in front of the eye'. This need not, in fact should not, be too deep. Its importance lies in expression, since it affects the placement of the eyes, and in the

fact that it defines the relative lengths of skull and muzzle. By
emphasizing the need for this definite stop, or break in the profile
of the face, the Standard ensures that the head shall be balanced.
Nothing is more ill-balanced and foreign to the breed than a
head which is longer in the foreface than the skull. When this
abnormality is met with there is usually no definite stop, merely
a slope down from a pair of offending bumps in the skull (of which
more later) towards the overlong muzzle. It is important to notice
that the Standard, in referring to a long head, alludes to 'length
of skull'. It does not specify any undue length of foreface. If we
refer back to the first Standard ever drawn up we find 'muzzle'
is described as 'most important, long and very powerful; no
approach to snipeyness'. This was no doubt deemed a desirable
recommendation at that time, for muzzles were in the main dis-
proportionately short and inclined to be pointed. The balanced

HEAD

3. Foreface too long   4. Skull longer than foreface

head with skull and muzzle of equal length, has since those days
become the accepted type and a characteristic feature of the
modern popular Scot. Those who drew up the modern Standard
knew better than to imply that the muzzle of itself could be
'powerful'. The muzzle in itself has no power whatever. The
strength of the jaws and gripping power is transmitted from the
muscles of the skull, which lie flat along the cheekbones. All that
is required of the muzzle from a power angle is that it should be
very strongly constructed, deep through, well filled up before the
eyes, and possess the large teeth indicated elsewhere in the
Standard. Greater length in skull than foreface is seldom seen
now, but where it exists, other details being correct, is infinitely
less objectionable than the reverse condition.

At the present time, possibly more than at any previous stage
of the breed's evolution, attention should be drawn to that
phrase in the Standard 'the length of skull enabling it to be
fairly wide and yet retain a narrow appearance'. It ought not

Ch. Heather Realisation

(Metcalfe)

Ch. Desco Desire

Ch. Walsing Wellborn

Int. Ch. Walsing Warrant

(Beeston Studios)

Ch. Medwal Miss Mustard

(Evelyn M. Shafer)

Int. Ch. Walsing Winning Trick in American Show ring

Ch. Niddbank Blue Print

Ortley Simon

Ch. Westpark Rio Grande

to be necessary to stress such an elementary truth for the know-ledgeable breeder as that 'appearance' is one thing and actual fact another. But modern trends seem to indicate either misinter-pretation of, or complete disregard for this section of the Standard, so that a little further elucidation may be desirable. We are told that the skull must be nearly flat and the cheekbones must not protrude. This means the top line of the skull when viewed in profile is practically a straight line from occiput to brow, and there must be no deviation from this straight line caused by bumps above and behind the brows. The sides of the skull must feel flat and possess a clean chiselled appearance without the protrusion of either cheekbones or flesh. This well-formed skull must at the same time be 'fairly wide'. When a skull is described as coarse, or thick, it is usually too broad in comparison to its length and its top and sides are both bumpy. This is a fault. So,

HEAD

5. Skull and foreface
correctly parallel

6. Bumpy skull

equally faulty, is the skull that is too narrow. It is all a matter of proportion. Retaining a narrow appearance means that the narrowness is only seeming and not real. We are not told that the skull should *appear* long; it must *be* long, its length enabl-ing it to be *fairly wide*. A fairly wide – and long – skull contri-butes to that look of wisdom and strength so characteristic of a typical Scot. We assume that such a dog has brains. A dog with an excessively narrow skull is apt to look foolish, and more often than not he is as big a fool as he looks. The point to be stressed is that it is not a case of the skull looking long because it is narrow, but looking narrow because it is long, which is a very different matter. A refectory table has a very narrow appearance as com-pared with other oblong tables, because its length is so much greater though its actual width may measure the same. A dog with a head of exceptional length throughout, skull and foreface being of equal proportions and other details correct, can often carry off a little extra width of skull successfully, over and above the

C

'fairly wide' skull indicated; where as the exceptionally narrow head cannot pass itself off as being of superlative length, and is the more serious failing of the two since it is contrary to the Standard and affects both eye and ear placement, and consequently expression, adversely.

When viewing the head in profile, it should be found that the nearly flat top line of the skull, if carried on in imagination to beyond the nose, is parallel to the top line of the muzzle. The

HEAD

7. Down-faced

8. Dish-faced

distance between such parallel lines is exactly equivalent to the depth of the stop. Such a profile ensures avoidance of either a down-face or a dish-face, and moreover is an important aid to correct eye-placement. Another characteristic feature, only appreciated in profile, is that the underline of the foreface should taper slightly towards the nose, which is in itself large. As the Standard says: 'in profile the line from the nose towards the

HEAD

9a. Correct projection of
nose over mouth

9b. Incorrect

chin appears to slope backwards'. This formation is a peculiarity of the breed and one that gives the head a character distinct from all other breeds of terrier. To the casual observer it is obliterated by beard and whisker, but the unique formation is a most important feature contributing to correct breed type.

The Standard tells us nothing regarding size of eyes, but it is universally accepted that the eyes should be small rather than large, though not so small as to resemble those of a pig. The main requirement is that they shall be set deeply under the brows, and be fairly wide apart. The width apart is in keeping with the fairly wide skull, and in actual fact when looking at a keenly alert dog full face, the distance between the haws, or inner corners of the eyes, should be approximately the same as that between the inner edges of the ears where they join the skull. Dark brown is the colour prescribed for the eyes, any tendency to a light shade being considered highly undesirable. Added to this they should be almond-shaped, never round. No one seems to have found a better description than almond-shaped to define the shape, but to give the correct expression the curve of the upper lid should be accentuated at a point a little nearer the haw than the centre, while the lower lid is a flat curve. Also the outer point of the eye should be slightly higher than the haw, or inner corner, so that at its broadest part the eye appears to be slightly oblique. It is essential for the eye to be so sunken under the brow that an imaginary line drawn from the upper to the lower lid would be vertical when the dog is looking straight ahead. This correct vertical setting has important bearing on expression and on the carriage of the head, for the dog's line of vision should be straight-forward along his nose, not looking upwards as if directed to the skies.

EARS

10. Correct   11. Incorrect   12. Too wide at base   13. Carried too wide

The size, shape, placement and carriage of the ears have an important bearing on expression and general appearance, which can be largely made or marred by them. Neat, sharply pointed erect ears adorn and give a finish to the head, adding to its look of alert intelligence. For a terrier kept originally for work there is no form of ear giving a greater protection to itself than a muscular prick ear, for with it the dog can close the two edges together and then bend them back to form a double fold. There should be enough ear to make this double fold completely effective as a guard, but not too much so as to be a vulnerable feature in a fight. Moderation in size should be the aim, as much for practical purposes as for appearance sake. Firmly erect and sharply pointed, the ears, when viewed from either front or back, form inverted V's, one line of which is perpendicular, the other sloping up to meet at the pointed tip. The essential requirement is that the perpendicular section of the V should be the outer edge of the ear, not the inner. It is an ugly fault when the ears converge towards each other or are too much on top of the head. The top of the head is not the place for them, they should be set on at the back and sides of the skull, but one might term the corner of the head. The lobes should not be pronounced. Viewed from the side with the dog looking keenly forward, the angle formed by the front edges of the ears and the top line of the skull should be just a little wider than a right angle. If tilted back further than this, or the dog's face carried at too downward an angle, the expression is plain and somewhat vapid. If the ears are too far forward, the expression becomes too much of a scowl.

EARS IN PROFILE

14. Correct relation to skull   15. Too far back   16. Too far forward

Before leaving the subject of heads, the only reliable way to measure their length is by calipers. Tape measurement gives fantastic results. One leg of the calipers is placed on the occiput, the other at the tip of the nose. With tape a domed or bumpy skull might increase measurement by as much as half an inch, but it would not be length. Where records are kept of head lengths (measured by calipers, of course) comparisons through the years can be very illuminating. It will be found that heads in the main are no longer now than twenty years ago. This may sound to some a very wild assertion, but it is true. Any seeming increase in length that has been made has taken place in the foreface at the expense of length of skull, while skilful trimming of the skull, throat and neck plus a profusion of whisker accentuates the over-all *appearance* of length.

The teeth should be large for a dog of the size, white and strong, the upper incisors fitting closely over the lower; and the four canines, or tusks, firmly interlocking. There should be six incisor teeth in each jaw, and both upper and lower should be sufficiently wide to allow every tooth to be evenly set. Small or cramped teeth or a narrow mouth are undesirable and should be penalized. So also should overshot or undershot mouths, though the former is a less serious fault than the latter and very often rights itself with age.

On the subject of neck the Standard is brief but to the point. The world 'muscular' implies strength, and 'of moderate length' leaves no room for misunderstanding, for the neck must be neither too short nor too long. There is more to it than that, however, too short a neck means want of liberty of movement; too long a neck implies muscular weakness. To a marked degree the neck should combine great strength with grace. It should taper slightly from the shoulders up to the head, and the slight

NECK

17. Correct; muscular, of moderate length

18. Too short, with straight shoulder

19. Too long

arch to the back line of the neck is typical of the correct outline of the dog, indicating muscular power. Of recent years a highly pernicious phrase has crept into use: 'reach of neck'. 'Reach' implies length; it also suggests something slender. Reach of neck is no doubt an admirable quality in a Greyhound or in any of the long-legged terrier breeds, but it should never be sought for nor applied to a Scottish Terrier, whose essential physical character is one of muscular sturdiness throughout. A nicely proportioned neck of moderate length, slightly tapering upwards but very muscular, carries the head at a proper angle, which is that of the line of head forming a right angle with the line of neck, the apex of such angle being slightly forward from the dog.

The fact that the second longest paragraph in the Standard is devoted to Forequarters shows of what great importance is this portion of the dog. Again we find mention of a muscular neck of moderate length, showing quality and set into a long sloping shoulder. Probably this part of the anatomy of a Scottish Terrier is less well understood than any. Good forequarters are unfortunately none too prevalent in the breed, and it seems certain details do not receive their fair share of attention from breeders and judges. The cry for short backs and straight forelegs at any price

20. Correct bone framework of forehand
(By kind permission of Dr C. Bremer.)

can cause the infinitely greater essentials of a muscular neck, sloping shoulder, the brisket well in front of the forelegs and the chest fairly broad, to get overlooked. The Scottish Terrier is of peculiar build, a build all his own, and his pronounced brisket, elbows well back, short sturdy legs and breadth of chest are some of his most typical characteristics. He requires to have a chamois-like balance and springing ability. His short legs lower his centre of gravity and enable him to scramble where a long-legged dog could not keep upright. The body should be slung between, and not placed on top of, the legs.

The connecting-links in the forehand are the scapula (shoulder-blade), the humerus (the bone connecting shoulder-blade to forearm), the forearm, and the pastern. On the relative position of the scapula, humerus and forearm depends the proper formation of the forehand. In the Scottish Terrier we require a long scapula and a comparatively short humerus. The scapula is

SHOULDER

21. Correct   22. Too straight

a long, flat, triangular bone, which should slope well back from below upwards, so that its topmost point (at the withers) is well to the rear of its lower end. At its lower end it joins the humerus, which, as has been said, should be short, and this forms the shoulders joint. The humerus should slope slightly downwards and backwards, which results in the elbow joint (where it meets the forearm) being well back, so ensuring the projecting brisket. If the angles formed by these joints are sufficienctly pronounced they result in what is known as a well-bent shoulder, as opposed to the too straight shoulder caused by the scapula and humerus both being too vertical. Viewed from the front, the elbows must not project outwards, nor be tucked under the body, but in action work fore and aft close to the ribs. If the chest be of the right breadth it will prevent the forelegs being too close together. Apropos of this, it was complete anathema to the late Mr. Robert Chapman to meet with what he termed a 'single Scottie', one in which, as he described it, 'both front legs came out of the same hole'!

Viewed from the side, the elbow joint should be definitely well behind the front line of the chest. From this set-back position the forearm descends vertically to the pastern and foot, and because of this characteristic construction of the forehand it has been truly said that in a good Scot there is almost as much of the dog in front of the forelegs as there is behind them. It is an exaggeration but a useful one, since it conveys the right idea.

FRONT

23. Correct   24. Too narrow   25. Pigeon-toed   26. Too bent
                                                              at pasterns

From the front view enough breadth of chest is desirable to conform to the Standard description of 'fairly broad'. It also indicates strength and plenty of lung space. The width of chest should allow a fairly large man's hand to be placed flat between the forelegs without touching them.

The forelegs should be big-boned, muscular, short from elbow to pastern, and appear straight when viewed from the front or the side. They should feel rounded to the touch, never flat or thin. This is the difference between what is usually alluded to as round bone and flat bone. Actually, bone has little to do with it, for the desired roundness is due to the way the sinews and muscles are laid on the leg. The forefeet should be big for the size of the dog, with very thick pads and well-arched firm toes. Thin, flat feet, or spread toes, are grave faults. The forefeet should complete the effect of a straight front by being neither turned inwards nor outwards.

The body shape is largely governed by the ribs, and a Scot should be big-ribbed for his size. The ribs should be well rounded where they leave the spine, and flatten to a deep chest. They should also be carried well back, thus ensuring plenty of lung and heart space. Attaining extra shortness of back has sometimes meant sacrificing good ribs. It is much more important that the dog should possess good deep ribs carried well back, with a strong muscular loin, than that he should measure an inch or so less from his withers to his tail. The two virtues are not entirely incompatible in any case, for examples can be found of dogs with good ribs both for depth and length, plus a strong muscular loin and yet withal short-backed and still agile. Such is the ideal, but excessively short bodies on a dog of such low build, on short legs, are apt to interfere with the fine, free, long-striding gait so typical of the breed. The loin should be very muscular, coupling the ribs to the hindquarters, and by its strength adds to the springing ability already alluded to. Pressure with the hand on the back of a well-constructed dog should meet with a strong, springy resistance. The Standard tells us that 'in general the top line of the body should be straight'. The favourite term is 'level top'. Though there is always an almost imperceptible rise towards the loin of a sturdy well-made dog, the aim is to avoid anything in the nature of a roach back, or a back showing any dip behind the shoulders.

The pelvis is a rigid bony structure firmly attached to the lower end of the spine. This, together with the upper and lower thigh bones and the lower leg, constitute the bony framework of the hindquarters. The Standard emphasizes the need for big and

HINDQUARTERS IN PROFILE

27. Good muscular thigh and well-bent stifle

28. Thin thigh and straight stifle

wide buttocks, and that the quarters should be remarkably powerful for the size of the dog. From its attachment to the pelvis at the hip joint, the upper thigh should slope sharply forwards and downwards to where it meets the lower thigh at the stifle (or knee joint). From the stifle the lower thigh slopes sharply backwards to the hock, which is the junction between the thigh and the lower leg. Covering the thighs there should be really powerful muscles. As has already been said, but can hardly be stressed too much, the well-bent stifle is enormously important and the keynote to correct breed type. The hock joint, too, should form an angle but not such an acute one as that formed at the stifle joint by the two thighs. The thighs should both look and feel very powerful, and be deep through from front to back when viewed in profile. Thin or shallow thighs ought to be regarded as an abomination. When the dog is standing keenly to attention, viewed from the side an imaginary line drawn from the rearmost part of the pelvis to the ground should just touch the hocks. Hocks stretched out further behind than this indicate weakness and an insufficient bend at both stifle and hock. Too much underneath the dog is just as faulty and suggests a bad mover. The lower leg, that is the portion from the hock to the foot, should stand vertically and be very short in comparison with the rest of the hindquarters. Hocks too far from the ground usually are associated with poor hind action. Looked at from behind, the hindquarters should convey great sturdiness, the hocks being neither converging towards each other (cow-hocked) nor being bowed wide apart. The hind feet are never quite as large as the forefeet, indeed should not be, but must be equally well padded and close-knit.

When seen to perfection, the movement of a good Scottish Terrier at trotting pace is one of the many characteristics which

HINDQUARTERS REAR VIEW

29. Correct   30. Cow-hocked   31. Bowed hocks

make him unique among short-legged breeds of dog. If forequarter and hindquarter construction are correct the whole movement of the dog, as the Standard indicates, will be smooth, easy and straightforward with free action at shoulder, stifle and hock. Moreover, he should take astonishingly long strides for a dog of his height and size. It is a good test of movement to discover how fast the dog can cover the ground without breaking into a canter or gallop. A really free-moving Scot can keep up a free trotting action at five miles per hour or more. When judging, movement can only be properly assessed by viewing the dog end-on, both coming and going, and also from the side. The propelling action of the hind legs should be apparent, with the hocks kept low; there should be no side-swing on the part of either leg, nor should the front legs be raised upwards with each step. The action is smooth, barely skimming the ground, the essential requirement being its long straightforward stride.

The tail is the termination of the spine, and as the Standard indicates should be of moderate length to give a general balance to the dog, both for practical and aesthetic purposes. It should be mobile and expressive. In shape it should feel very thick at the root, and taper to a point at the tip. During my lifelong connection with the breed I have always found the thick root to the tail to be one of the surest indications of vigour and stamina, and it is a feature to be looked for even in the youngest of puppies. In carriage it should be upright in general effect, but this does not mean that where it leaves the back the angle formed by the back and the tail is a sharp one. It should be a little wider than a right

TAIL

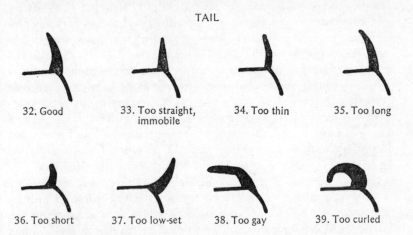

32. Good   33. Too straight, immobile   34. Too thin   35. Too long

36. Too short   37. Too low-set   38. Too gay   39. Too curled

angle, and the slight curve permissible towards the ears of the dog, provides the upright appearance. A rigidly straight tail looks unnatural and is seldom as mobile and useful for balance as one with a gentle curve. Any bend either sideways or backwards instead of the normal way forwards, is highly undesirable, as also is an over-gay tail carried too much along the dog's back; while a definitely curly tail is, in more senses than one, 'the end'. Moderate should be the aim for length, as a tail either too long or too short is disproportionate to the rest of the dog, the latter failing being the worse for it arouses suspicions that some portion of it has been removed. Occasionally some puppies are born with a kink in some part of the tail. Unless this is very accentuated and causes an alteration in the carriage of the tail it is not a serious blemish.

The coat is mentioned twice in the Standard, and as stated should be close-lying and double. The words 'broken and rough-textured' are sometimes misinterpreted; broken is merely an indication that it is a rough coat as opposed to a smooth one, while rough-textured refers to the harsh feel of the outercoat and does not mean a rough appearance. The undercoat is not normally seen, except when the dog is in process of shedding his outercoat or being stripped, or when the coat is ruffled up by hand during examination for texture. As a weather-resisting covering and protection against injury this furry undercoat is of the utmost importance and should be present all over the body. Its density should make it quite difficult to divide the hair by hand enough to see the skin of the dog, and it is practically impervious to moisture. Every hair comprising the harsh, wiry outercoat should be straight. In consequence the coat lies flat and fits the dog closely. Any tendency to wave or curl is highly undesirable. A really good-coated dog with the same hard-textured hair covering the legs right down to the toes is a joy to possess, whatever job he is called upon to fill. As a worker he will not have a lot of shaggy long hair to get plastered with mud and entangled in undergrowth; as a companion and house-dog he will not come in out of the wet looking utterly bedraggled and dripping moisture wherever he goes, but dries off quickly; while as a show dog his hard coat will be deemed a virtue by all right-thinking judges. Buyers of young stock would be well advised to insist upon the harder-coated specimens. As puppies they may look the plainest and smoothest in a litter, but ample furnishings will develop with maturity. Most people, if they stopped to think, would prefer their dog when adult to be easily kept clean and tidy by means of a daily brushing, and to look a typical representative of his breed rather than an animated wool-bag. If the fuzzy-faced woolly coated pup has a special appeal, far better buy a Poodle.

The hair on the foreface has always been characteristically longer than elsewhere and is a wise provision of Nature as a protection when at work. For show purposes it is the fashion to cultivate this face hair to excess, and provided it is not soft and silky in texture or so long as to sweep the floor or to make the dog look grotesque it can do but little harm and even finds favour in the eyes of some judges.

When our breed joined the ranks of those which have to be trimmed for show, coats deteriorated somewhat as was only to be expected. Such deterioration has proved to be more a matter of too much profusion of coat rather than loss of texture. Every adult Scot looks the better for a judicious amount of slightly longer coat under the body, down the legs and on the foreface. These are called furnishings and it is a natural growth in moderation. But at one time, after the Second World War, such furnishings were encouraged beyond all reason so that the breed was a laughing-stock in the show-ring with its beard, frills, leg-hair and 'valances' trailing the ground. None of such long hair could ever be described as harsh or wiry, but its profusion offered scope for the skilful trimmer to carve the outline into any shape he wished, and so long as the dog did not get wet or stand in a gale of wind its 'hair-do' would remain intact and an insult to a working breed. Fortunately the judges very soon got wise to the fact that such fantastic presentation was used solely to cover up structural defects, and let us hope that present-day and future owners will never set eyes on such peculiar misapplication of the art of trimming, for modern show presentation is in the main more reasonable. Harsh outercoats are still inherent in the breed and should be selected for as one of the essentials towards universal popularity. Overlong too profuse hair is invariably of soft texture and therefore has no place on the hardy workmanlike Scottish Terrier.

It does not seem to be generally known what a very wide range of coat colours exist in the breed. The Standard reference to colour is terse but comprehensive. 'Black, wheaten, or brindle of any colour' embraces the whole series of gloriously varying colours present and permissible. The only thing a Scottish Terrier must not be is colourless, for white is disallowed. In its early days white chest patches and white toes were very prevalent in the breed, and even today a few white hairs are occasionally found on the chest. This is not a serious fault as they generally disappear with maturity, but are undesirable if present to any extent. The definition of the word brindle is brown with streaks of other colour, but in dogs the term is applied somewhat loosely to all coats which are not of one self-colour throughout. Thus we get brown-brindle, grey-brindle, red-brindle, golden-brindle and black-brindle (this last being mainly black in appearance but has an intermingling of brown hairs). The absolute self-colours are black, red, or wheaten. Only a small proportion of the breed's most famous winners have been jet black. Blacks had a great run of popularity from about 1922 for ten years or so, as the majority of top winners just at that time were either black or black-brindle. Naturally the fact that Ch. Albourne Admiration and Ch. Heather Necessity happened to be blacks also did much to foster public interest in this colour. A really clear red all over (the colour of an Irish Terrier) is unusual but does occur occasionally. They generally have touches of black, or dark shadings on face, ears, and tail. The wheatens vary too in the amount of darker shading present. Some are evenly the colour of ripe corn throughout, as in Ch. Medwal Wild Oats, whereas others with a basis of wheaten colour have a strong admixture of black-tipped hairs and are therefore sometimes described as wheaten-brindles. Some of them should more properly be called red-wheatens, as was Ch. Medwal Miss Mustard. As yet there have been only six wheaten champions, but in the last two or three years the colour is making a fresh bid for popularity and can claim many adherents in America and Canada. So many terms are used to describe the endless varieties of coat-colour, often the same shade receiving many contrasting descriptions. A light shade of grey, which some call silver brindle, is not seen so often today as it used to be. Well-known specimens of this colour have been Marksman of Docken, Ch. Tweburn Clincher, and Ch. Reimill Realist. A dark, or iron-grey, conveys a serviceable look at granite hardness and is nearly always linked with good texture. Ch. Live Wire and Ch. Broxton Blaze were of this shade. One of the most all-round useful colours, and pleasing withal, is a warm red brindle. It was much favoured in the old days for the dogs which were worked and is invariably weather-resisting. There have been many red-brindle celebrities, not the least among them being Albourne Annie Laurie, Ch. Walsing Whisper, Ch. Walsing Wellborn and Ch. Heather Benefactor. Some would describe light red brindles as sandy brindles, and under this category have come Ch. Glencannie Red Robin, Ch. Brantvale Boilin' O'er, and Ch. Ortley Sandy. The winner of more Challenge Certificates in the breed than any dog yet, Ch. Heather Realisation, was a medium shade of grey brindle in colour, and it may be well to note that of the first hundred champions in the breed since the Second World War, seventy-five per cent have been of colours other than black, ranging from light to dark variations. In view of this it seems strange that the British public, when setting out to buy a Scot, appears to cherish the conviction that black is the only possible and correct colouring. It is thought that the familiar display posters advertising a certain brand of whisky have been largely responsible for this odd misconception. It would be just as reasonable to argue that all horses, all greyhounds and all poodles must be black, for with the exception only of white the Scot's range of coat colours is just as wide as in those species of animal. As is so often quoted, a good dog, like a good horse, cannot be a bad colour.

5

Character

IT is assumed that every reader of this book will know to some extent what a Scottish Terrier looks like, and the various illustrations will confirm that it is the same rugged-looking, low-to-ground fellow who, when met with on the street is invariably addressed by passers-by as 'Scottie' or 'Jock' or 'Mac'. But the reader may not be conversant with the unique character within. Only those who have at some time possessed a Scottish Terrier, or been possessed by one, can realize the privilege it is to study and try to understand a personality of such depth.

The description in detail of what a perfect specimen should look like has already been given, but even though a dog does not comply wholly with this description he may none the less be a Scottish Terrier. Though he may be faulty in many external details he will possess certain distinguishing characteristics common to the whole of his species. He will be a comparatively short-legged little dog with a harsh coat, erect ears, watchful eyes, and a head which looks big for his size, plus the mentality peculiar to his race. And this is the greatest thing about him, for his nature is as unique as his physical appearance. It is a nature that does not appeal to all and sundry. The Scot himself has no wish that it should. He does not curry favour, nor does he bestow his affections lightly, but once given his devotion is unswerving and lifelong.

So different is he from other breeds, with contours and character all his own. He is the philosopher among dogs, aloof, reserved dignified and very independent. He has the tact, unassuming self-confidence, patience, tolerance and understanding of a true gentleman. His instinctive tendency towards good manners make him the perfect companion. As a discriminating judge of human nature he has few equals. He will weigh you up and either treat you with supreme indifference, or indicate by his manner that he accepts you. To merit the approbation of a typical Scottish Terrier is a sign of grace, while to deserve and win his respect and loyalty is to know one of the best meanings of the word friend.

His presence in a household can never be ignored; his immense understanding of and interest in all that goes on make him a personality in every house in which he finds a home, and there is no breed possessing to the same degree that sympathy with and understanding of humans. When he takes up residence in a new home be he puppy or adult, he usually adopts one person in particular, being essentially a one-man dog, but at the same time by the sheer force of his personality he very quickly has every member of the household exactly where he wants them.

The real nature of a typical Scot is shown by nothing more clearly than the very rare use he makes of his bark, his organ of speech. Like his human counterpart, the Celt, he is not given to idle chatter or small talk. Unless very badly brought up he is not perpetually barking at trifles. When he does bark it is only after due deliberation as to its necessity. He soon learns what he can obtain by means of his speech, but he reserves it for when he requires it and then very plainly expresses a desire or an opinion. This is just one of his many pleasing qualities. He mostly takes life as it comes, contentedly and without protest. In him you have a stout-hearted pal, hardy enough to share all the ups and downs of life, tough enough and willing to accompany you anywhere at any time, keep going all day if need be, fitted to withstand hardship with stoical endurance, adaptable and intelligent above the ordinary. He knows when he is not wanted, never forces himself upon you and never complains.

Game to the very last, he is blessed with a keen nose, good sight and the most acute hearing, and instinctively loves doing the work for which he originally existed, that of hunting and digging for vermin both above and below ground. As a burrower he uses his big teeth as well as his paws and makes a quick job of it. Among his own clan he is usually peace-loving and does not pick quarrels unnecessarily, but if Fate decrees that a battle has to be fought he lays hold with a determination never to let go and would die in the struggle rather than give in or run away. This strength of character earned him his old title of Diehard. Having a strong sense of possession he will defend his own territory and stand his ground if challenged, and thinks nothing of tackling an intruder four or five times his own size when occasion demands.

The American novelist S. S. Van Dine, who at one time had a successful kennel of Scottish Terriers, wrote that the Scot is 'one of the few dogs with whom human beings can actually argue'. And how true that is. One can carry on a conversation with one's Scot pal and it is not as one-sided as might be imagined, for the twitch of an ear, the expression in his eyes, and maybe a slight movement of the tip of his tail will tell you he has not only listened to every word you said but has understood; which is more than can be said for a lot of one's human acquaintances! In fact, the more you credit him with the wisdom he possesses and talk to him like the reasoning individual he is, the more intelligent and responsive does he become and the more pleasure do you get from knowing him.

As for argument, some people dub him obstinate, even perverse. But naturally such a wise dog has a mind of his own; he thinks for himself and he reasons things out, and if in his eminently commonsense view he considers you are in the wrong he can be as stubborn as only a Scotsman nows how. He will obey grudgingly in such case (and at his own speed), but when mutual respect and understanding exist between owner and dog he senses your very thoughts almost before they have taken shape and has an innate desire to please. Harsh words or punishment get you absolutely nowhere with him; such treatment only makes him morose and even shy, or drives him into displaying an even greater show of his natural independence.

One of the most endearing qualities about a Scottish Terrier is his sense of humour. From his earliest puppyhood he can see the funny side of himself, his playmates and his human companions, and the typical Scots keeps a sense of playfulness right on into old age. He hates, like any dog, to be laughed *at*, but there is nobody better than he to enjoy a joke *with*. There seem no limits to his originality. As quite a young pup he is full of fresh notions, and will improvise games for himself, and if given a few of the right sort of playthings can amuse himself for hours. If not repressed but cultivated along sensible lines he can be taught to do anything of which any dog is capable, and to enjoy being taught.

Exceptionally clever people have very keen perceptions and are highly sensitive, and the Scot is no exception since the word human is the only one which adequately describes his nature. One of his distinctive characteristics is a definite self-consciousness. He hates to be watched and he hates to be stared at, seeming to resent the intrusion upon his independence of thought or action. It was said that Sir Edward Elgar used to watch his dogs at play through a mirror, so that they could not see they were being watched, and with a bunch of Scots who conjure up games among themselves it will be found nine times out of ten if you take up a position to watch the fun they will quit playing at once and pretend utter indifference. There is no dog more clever at suddenly registering that look of complete aloofness, seeming to look through you or past you into space, and properly 'putting you in the farthing seats'.

Never any gushing and excitement on the part of a true Scot if you have been away on a visit without him and left him to the tender mercies of others. He will have missed you but would scorn to show it, and in his philosophical manner just makes the best of what comes his way in your absence and never frets. Should his gladness at your return cause him to display ever so little exuberance, he will suddenly appear self-conscious, wear a preoccupied look and appear to repent having let his feelings get the better of him. But in his quiet way he will stick around thereafter and take possession of you again.

If he trusts and respects you and you are fortunate enough to have won his undying affection, he will reflect your mood, and his watchful eyes will read your every expression. He shares your every emotion; if you are gay he rejoices inwardly and with decent restraint; if you are sad there is no one more sympathetic and understanding than he. The use he makes of his ears alone can express more than most people's countenances, while he has no need of words to put over to you the innumerable meanings his eyes can convey. Thoreau's words were not written about a dog, but they apply to our beloved Scot. 'The language of friends is not words but meanings. It is an intelligence above language.'

6

General Management

WHETHER one keeps but one Scottish Terrier or more, there are certain principles to be observed regarding their management in order to get the greatest enjoyment, or profit, or both, from one's dogs. There is no point in acquiring pure-bred stock unless one is prepared to spend both time and money keeping it in the best possible condition.

First and foremost, every dog deserves to be kept healthy, and to be kept happy. The one state is largely dependant on the other, for an ailing dog is a misery to himself as well as to his owner and cannot enjoy life, while an unhappy dog will sooner or later become a sick dog. It is a dog's nature to keep himself fit, but sometimes the misguided attentions of a fond owner, or the ignorance of a careless one, or neglect of some of the basic principles of sound management, are reponsible for disorders that need never have arisen. Good management results from a real love of a dog, a slight knowledge of hygiene, an ability to look ahead, and strict attention to details. One's aim should be rather to assist Nature than make attempts to improve upon it. Too much dosing, too much artificiality, or what may be termed over-civilization in the care of the dogs only leads to trouble, but reasonable care and attention to detail allied to common sense and forethought should maintain a well-reared Scot clean, happy and healthy all the days of his life until the natural decay of old age sets in. The essential factors towards good managment may be classified under five headings: housing, feeding, exercise, training and grooming.

Housing

Every dog requires a bed of his own in which he can sleep cosily at night and to which he can retire during the day if he so wishes. Whether a house-dog or kennel-dog it is most important that his bed be should well raised above floor level. Even the best constructed houses or kennel buildings have floor draughts, and no one should be surprised at house-dogs selecting the best armchairs to sit in if they have not been provided with draught-proof beds of their own. Adult Scots can stand a lot of cold, but cannot prosper if expected to sleep in a draught. Draughts come from overhead as well as along the floor, consequently the best sort of bed is a covered raised box open only at one end. Let this entrance to the box be of the same dimensions as the interior, to facilitate easy cleaning, and have a moveable ledge along the front to keep the bedding in place. For indoor dogs a pad or cushion made of clean sacking and filled with wood-wool or shavings and fitting the box, makes a wholesome mattress, over which, anyway in winter-time, a blanket or small rug can be spread. Blankets used for the indoor bed should be washable and changed at least once a week, while at regular longer intervals the stuffed cushion should be renewed. It is essential the dog's bed should be kept as clean as one's own.

Similar shaped sleeping-boxes are suitable for use in out-buildings or kennels, and in this case it is even more urgent to have them raised well up from the floor. Ten to fifteen inches above floor level is appreciated by adult dogs. It will always be found when a Scot is housed in an outbuilding he will climb on to the highest thing available to sleep, so it is best to provide that which helps to keep him happy and is draught-free. Many kennel-makers now supply various types of indoor kennels, or hutches, with barred door or fronts, and any dog-owner with some idea of simple carpentering can make these for himself. Several can be built in one unit along a suitable indoor wall, and provided such closed pens are used intelligently and not abused there is a lot to recommend them. They economize space, for more dogs can be housed under one roof at night which means they generate warmth and will sleep more contentedly. Moreover they facilitate feeding; easier for the person serving out the food, and this plan ensures that each occupant eats separately and uninterruptedly and can be left shut in until he has finished. To avoid noise and disturbed nights, do not arrange such pens opposite each other, or where the occupants can see other dogs. My own wall-pens are built in one row, raised fifteen inches from the floor so that the space underneath them is not wasted, when the dogs are free to roam around. Each dog soon gets to know its own pen, and at feeding-time each jumps into his own compartment in eager expectation of his meal. It will be found they often show a distinct preference for this type of abode, and though out of sight of each other when shut in for the night seem to appreciate the sense of companionship provided by the close proximity of their next-door neighbours. The inside measurement of each such pen should never be less than 2 ft. 6 in. in all directions, and they should be smoothly constructed so that there are no cracks or crevices to harbour dirt. The barred front gates to each should have strong and fool-proof fastenings.

The main consideration in regard to such small pens is that they must not on any account be used except as feeding-places and sleeping-places. A short night of never more then seven hours' duration, preferably only six, is as much as any dog should be asked to endure in such a confined space, and provided he has been well exercised in the forenoon and is allowed some freedom the rest of the day, a couple of hours' afternoon nap in his pen is sometimes useful. But Scottish Terriers do not prosper with perpetual or too frequent imprisonment. Their independent natures and keen interest in all happenings make human company essential to their well-being, and where the dogs are allowed to lead a free happy life sharing the house, garden, and various activities of the owner, their individuality can be expressed and they always do best in consequence. Every day should provide an opportunity for every dog to develop its personality in this way. But wall-pens in the right hands can serve a purpose. They are not for the lazy lie-a-bed type of owner, for the dogs need and expect to be released at daybreak. Neither are they suitable houseing for in-whelp bitches or puppies. It is a fairly well-known fact that neither dogs nor bitches will soil their own beds, consequently the judicious use of a pen of this kind for training towards housecleanliness has an obvious value. But a warning should be issued against confining any male dog for too long a period in such a pen, for they as a rule are far more meticulous than bitches in this respect, and if confined for any longer than seven hours at the most may not only suffer agonies of discomfort but are likely to develop kidney or bladder trouble. Therefore an essential part of sane management if small sleeping-pens are used is a late-night opportunity for every dog to relieve itself, and some healthy early rising on the part of their attendant. For terriers being prepared for show, wall-pens have their uses, partly from a psychological angle which will be dealt with later under show training, and partly because the more frequent human handling involved encourages the dog's confidence in its handler.

A well-ordered breeding establishment will have various types of kennel accommodation to suit all classes and ages of stock; separate quarters well away from the rest of the pack for bitches in season; a puppy house with large, light, airy and dry space for playrooms; possibly a separate dog's kitchen; and secluded quiet accommodation for whelping pitches. Roomy stalls with gates, after the style of loose-boxes, make good accommodation for all ages, provided they are dry, light and well ventilated, and permit space for the sleeping-box or bench plus enough room for the dog or a couple of dogs to move about freely. In such stalls, open raised benches can be used for sleeping in summer, but cosy boxes are necessary in winter and either should be well raised above floor level. Whatever type of housing is used remember that a dwelling within a dwelling, or several pens or stalls under one roof, are far more satisfactory than single outside wooden structures. If there is no alternative to using some of the latter, they should be lined throughout roof and walls, and it is advisable to fill the double walls with sawdust. Otherwise, unless fitted with artificial heating of some kind, they are far too subject to climatic changes of temperature, miserably cold in winter and painfully hot in summer.

Only the very aged and the very young of our breed require artificial heat in their dwellings under normal conditions, but it is well to be prepared with some accommodation which can be heated in emergencies, especially a place for isolating any cases of sickness or suspected sickness. The main danger about dogs sleeping in too warm an atmosphere is the sudden change of temperature to which they are subjected when let outdoors. To allow a house-dog to bake in front of a hot fire all evening and then put him in a cold place to sleep savours of distinct cruelty. Changes of temperature should be made gradually.

Wood is the best substance for all kennel floors. If an existing building with brick or concrete floors is converted into kennels, always provide large boarded sections laid down over the greater part of the floor. All such sections, and all boxes and benches should be easily removable for cleaning and all woodwork ought to be well impregnated with creosote. This preserves the wood and discourages vermin and prevents urine soaking in. It is well to give a fresh coat of creosote annually, but never place a dog into a freshly creosoted stall or box until the dressing has dried off and lost some of its smell. Someone once made a happy 'Spoonerism' by quoting 'Cleanliness is next to Dogliness', and nothing could be more true, for every portion of every kennel and sleeping-box should be kept scruptulously clean. For kennel bedding some owners use wood-wool, some use clean wheat straw, some use plain sackcloth and some newspaper. Whatever bedding is used, give a generous quantity of it in cold weather, and every day the sleeping-boxes should be emptied, well brushed out, and the bedding, or a fresh supply of it, replaced. If blankets or sacks are used, have a plentiful supply at hand, so that one set can be in use while others are in the wash-tub. Be very sure no dog is ever supplied with damp bedding.

Every stall, shed, kennel or building in which dogs are housed should be subjected to a thorough sweep-out daily, with special attention to corners. A nearly dry long-handled mop which has been soaking in disinfectant and then well squeezed out can freshen up the floors after sweeping and before a little dry sawdust is sprinkled down. But the mopping should be done as dryly as possible and when the dogs can stay out of their kennels awhile so that they do not return to a damp floor. A certain amount of sawdust on the floors facilitates cleaning and helps to keep the floors dry. But never use sawdust in a kennel where puppies under three months are housed. Newspapers spread always in the same corner of their abode makes a far safer 'lavatory' for them. Before that age they have no discretion as to what is fit to eat and what is not, and serious trouble can arise from pups consuming it deliberately or getting it mixed up with their food by accident. If sensible tactics are followed and a daily routine adhered to by the fact of the items in each stall being regularly put in the same place – such as box in one corner, water-bowl in another and a patch of sawdust in a third – it will be found the dogs prefer to use the sawdust patch for its appointed purpose, and thus much labour is saved when cleaning and no sawdust gets into the water-bowl. All dogs kennelled for several hours in one place should have a supply of fresh clean drinking-water, and it is advisable to use the non-spillable type of bowl for the purpose. Some have an irritating habit of playing with water-bowls, either digging in them with their paws or pushing them around with their noses, resulting in water being everywhere except the right place. This sort should be handed a drink of water at stated intervals instead of leaving it with them. It is a habit they usually grow out of, luckily.

Whatever disinfectants are used, avoid those containing carbolic. There are several good safe veterinary disinfectants on the market. Some owners prefer to use none at all but to depend upon regular scrubbing of all woodwork with soft soap and water. Any method is sound that results in perfect cleanliness and a sweet-smelling atmosphere in the kennels. No excreta or damp sawdust should ever be left lying around, and a few dogs with extra dirty habits may keep a kennel assistant busy with shovel and brush at all hours of the day, for the aim should be that the whole place is sweet and clean and fit to be seen by visitors at any time.

The space available governs to some extent the aspect and ground-plan of kennels, but if possible arrange that they face south-east or south, that they are sheltered from north and east winds, are built on good foundations and well raised above ground-level. A covered yard for exercise in wet weather is a valuable addition to a large kennel. The main open-air yard may be as big as space permits provided it is not too large to be kept clean at all times. The best boundary for such yard is something solid through which the dogs cannot see. Nothing beats a permanent brick or stone wall, not less than four feet in height on the sunny side and six feet or more towards the north side, but if this is not possible a fence of solid timber can be just as effective though not so lasting and requires regularly creosoting. An open wire boundary has too many drawbacks, but if it has to be resorted to, small-mesh chain link or something similar, erected very taut, is the only safe type of wire fencing. Solid boundaries discourage unnecessary noise, for if dogs are left in a wired yard too long they will be on the lookout for anything they can see, to relieve their boredom, and probably develop a barking habit. Moreover many Scots are clever climbers, and some can negotiate a four-foot wire-mesh fence like a cat. Ordinary gauge wire netting is useless. There isn't anything our breed does not know about getting through or burrowing under wire netting. Especially is it dangerous where puppies play, for a strand of wire often works loose and the pups tumbling against it during their games can sustain serious injury to eyes or ears.

A main communal yard, on to which all the main kennel buildings lead, is found to be a practicable and happy arrangement for Scots. They are all the better for mixing with their friends, relations and neighbours during part of each day and if the whole kennel population does not agree well enough to run together while the work of kennel-cleaning and grooming is in progress, smaller batches of a few at a time can take turns enjoying the freedom of the yard. The surface of the yard should be either concrete or brick or stone paving of some kind over the greater part. Concrete is popular and, if well laid, permanent. Personally, I have found sand-faced hand-made bricks better, being just as good for the terrier's feet and not so cold a surface in winter. Some use asphalt, but this becomes painfully hot in sunny weather. A cheap form of yard surface can be made from kiln-ash, a deep layer of which is put down over a previously prepared foundation of clinker and broken brick to aid drainage. Whatever material is used, the yard should slope sufficiently to allow all moisture to drain off, and if fitted with a proper drain so much the better so that the whole place can be hosed at intervals in suitable weather.

A few smaller runs will be necessary for puppies, which cannot as a rule mix safely with the adults. If not attached to the puppies' own living place, such runs must always be supplied with a weather-proof covered box or a small portable kennel in which the pups can take refuge when they want. But no puppies should be left long enough in open-air runs to get sleepy, tired, or bored. A litter, or a batch of pups of similar age, will amuse themselves for quite a time, but as soon as they quit playing or running around briskly, bring them in. And reserve such runs solely for the use of groups of pups. Adult dogs left in small runs are miserably unhappy objects and are doing themselves no good. Far better be kenelled in their dry stalls or indoor pens, in between spells of freedom when they can keep busily active all the time.

Even if an owner is so peculiar as to like unnecessary noise or to be oblivious of it when it occurs, there are frequently neigh-bours in the vicinity of a kennel with whom it is as well to keep on friendly terms. Therefore the same rule applies to outdoor runs as to indoor pens – do not arrange them so that the inmates see each other. It merely leads to silly excitability – and quite possibly fighting – on the part of the young stock, while adults so kennelled will quickly degenerate from the quiet restrained breed they are by nature into a crazy bunch of barkers. It is not their fault if they do. If and when a kennel of Scots is noisy, it is either the result of mismanagement or bad kennel-planning, or both. Unnecessary noise is a thing to be discouraged in any kennel; it benefits neither dog nor man and irritates many. Particularly is it out of character with our self-possessed philo-sophic breed. So the point is worth keeping in mind when plan-ning the layout of the kennels. An additional advantage, where space permits, is a rough grass run, field or paddock (or it may have to be the owner's garden) leading off from the main yard, into which the dogs can be let for occasional gallops where they can really stretch their legs and expand their lungs.

Essential though it is that the aspect of the kennels should derive all the sunshine possible, it is equally important that the midday heat of summer sunshine should be tempered somewhat by light shade from some deciduous trees near the permanent buildings and the main yards. It is definitely cruel to shut a dog in a sun-baked restricted space when the weather is hot. One of the best trees for the purpose is a small-leaved silver birch, for it can be planted when six to eight feet tall, is quick-growing, and casts a not too dense shade in midsummer; while its tiny leaves are no trouble in the fall and its bare branches keep back none of the all-too-rare winter sunshine and cause very little drippage after rain.

Feeding

Food should be given only at regular hours. The best routine for adult dogs is a light snack in the morning and the main meal in the evening. This is in harmony with Nature, for a dog's instinct is to sleep soundly after his appetite has been satisfied. Puppy-feeding is discussed in Chapter 8. Remember that feed-ing-time is a big moment in a dog's day; he looks forward to it.

So see to it that all feeding-pans are clean, that the main meal is well prepared and in winter-time given slightly warm (just chill-off). Extravagance is unnecessary. As with all other commodities the best is the cheapest in the long run, so be sure all foods used are of best quality. It is a big mistake to think just anything will do for the dog, if he is both to look and feel fit and happy. The staple foods should be lean meat and wholemeal bread. Supplementary items are raw eggs, fresh milk, rabbit flesh, sheep's heads and paunches, offals such as tongue, hearts and kidneys (be wary of using too much liver), large beef-bones and *very* occasionally fish. Also there is considerable value in finely chopped *raw* cabbage, raw carrot, watercress and parsley, which can in turn be added to the main meal with advantage. Cooked vegetables are of no food value to dogs, and they seldom like them anyway. Never feed potatoes to dogs.

The meat should be mainly lean, fresh and of good colour. Beef is the most usual. Mutton, if it can be got, is more fattening if a certain dog requires specially building up. If horseflesh is used, it should be fed more sparingly than beef, otherwise it has a scouring effect. The brown, or wholemeal bread should all be turned into rusks, which are prepared by slicing the loaf and baking in a slow oven until crisp and golden brown. These can be stored in quantity in an air-tight tin and will keep almost indefinitely. They are of greater food value than most forms of biscuit meal, but in a large kennel it may be necessary to stock some of the latter. Again, be particular about quality, and if in doubt seek the advice of an experienced breeder as to the best brands; store it in dry air-proof bins and use sparingly. The morning snack can be either a rusk, or a hard crisp dog-biscuit of terrier size and again of a recommended variety. The dogs appreciate and expect something of this sort after their first morning outing, and the dry crispness of rusk or biscuit helps to keep their teeth clean.

Raw eggs are extremely valuable for stud dogs, nursing mothers, invalids and growing puppies. They should be offered beaten up in a little warm milk and preferably sweetened with honey, or can be added to the main meal. Milk is seldom needed as a regular part of an adult dog's menu, but is a grand conditioner for those requiring a build-up, helpful to the still growing youngsters of around a year old, and necessary for the invalids or the aged. Many owners go the round of the kennels last thing at night giving every inmate a wee drink of warm milk; they certainly love it and it suits most indviduals. For the junior under eighteen months of age, a dish of warm milk after the morning rusk is beneficial.

When rabbit is fed to dogs, it must be extra well boiled so that the flesh literally falls off the bones, and the most meticulous care must be taken in preparing the meal that no bones whatever are fed to the dog. Go through it twice to make doubly sure. The same remarks apply to sheep's heads, for any bones which have been cooked are most dangerous. Sheep's paunches, well boiled, or bullock's tripe, cleaned before being cooked, make a welcome change of diet and are easily digestible. They have a use for tempting a dainty feeder or for dogs recovering from an illness, but should not be viewed as a staple diet or a substitute for good red meat. The so-called offals, hearts, tongues, etc., need well boiling and make the resulting broth good and nourishing, which can be used later for moistening either rusk or biscuit meal. Liver is too apt to cause diarrhoea, unless used very sparingly. Be careful never to feed any gristle among the meat – it can cause fits.

As regards bones, the only sort really desirable and good for a dog are beef shin-bones, always given raw. Get the butcher to saw these through into three or four sections, not smash them, then carefully remove any small chips of bone that may be attached, and also remove the larger lumps of gristle before giving the bone to the dog. The best time for him to have it is after his supper, and he *must* be kennelled alone the while. Such bones are necessary for keeping the teeth in good order, besides being a form of entertainment for the dog. As he will derive quite a bit of nourishment from a fresh one, give him a smaller supper on 'bone night'. In the morning be very sure all bones are picked up and removed before the dogs run together, and of course no bones should ever be left lying around the main yard or playground. After gnawing a bone a dog is extra thirsty, and this brings us to the essential business of fresh drinking-water being easily accessible at all times. Healthy dogs drink a lot of water, and the drinking-bowls must be replenished at all times of day. For dogs sleeping in wall-pens it is not always possible to provide a fixed water-trough, but as has been emphasized earlier, seven hours at the most is the longest time any dog should be shut in, and he must have access to water immediately on emerging in the morning.

Fish is more of a cat-food than a dog-food and if used often will inevitably start skin trouble. The most useful sort is fresh herring, well boiled to a mash, the heads and backbones removed, and the remainder mingled with some rusks or biscuit meal. They help to fatten when this is needed, but should not be given more than once a week.

If well organized and judicious use is made of the afore-mentioned foods, dog-feeding is quite simple, but a few points must be stressed. One is, dry food at the main meal. Never give sloppy wet stuff. If biscuit meal or rusks have been soaked in the broth resulting from the cooking of the meat, make sure it has had only enough broth added to dry off into a crumbly condition. A dog's natural diet if he could get it would be raw flesh, so as often as circumstances and your meat supply permit, feed the beef raw, cut up into small pieces. To vary matters it is a good plan to alternate between raw meat, boiled meat, and baked or roasted meat. As to the amount, an average Scot adult requires about three-quarters of a lb. of lean meat per day.

Into the pot in which the meat is boiled add an onion. Its effect is beneficial against worms. Additions can be made to the main meal such as cod-liver oil in winter, Bemax at any time, and a weekly dose of liquid paraffin on the food suits many dogs. But the wise owner will soon discover the variations and idio-syncrasies of individual dogs, and feed each accordingly. The novice owner should be warned against overfeeding, for the Scottish Terrier is a greedy feeder by nature, and will usually eat all he is offered and still ask for more. If allowed all he can take, as happens to some pet dogs, the inevitable result is skin trouble. The breed has absolutely no more tendency to skin disorders than any other breed, and if such arise it is usually the owner's fault. But bearing in mind the Scot's natural greed, it is well to find out what amounts keeps each dog in the best possible condition, and ration the dog accordingly to that amount of food. No Scottish Terrier can look its best if thin. On the other hand surplus fat is unhealthy, and in bitches required for breeding can cause a lot of trouble. One should aim for a happy medium, a dog well covered and nicely rounded with firm flesh and muscle.

A final warning to the novice owner about choking, or the

habit some dogs have of getting food stuck in the roof of the mouth. It is the result of unsuitably sticky food or feeding them unrusked bread, or the very small-sized type of biscuit marketed by several firms. These can get wedged in the roof of the mouth; the dog then appears to be trying to stand on his head, clawing frantically at the sides of his mouth in an effort to dislodge the obstruction. If he is among his kennel-mates at the time they will all set upon him unless human aid quickly pushes the obstruction backwards towards the wider part of his mouth and frees it. A lot of unnecessary kennel fights start this way.

So feed sanely, feed regularly, feed dry, and always remove the dish after a reasonable time whether the dog has cleaned it or not. Never leave food with him in the hope he will eat it later. And remember at all times the supply of fresh clean drinking-water.

Exercise

To maintain good health, every dog requires daily exercise. What form this exercise takes may have to be governed in part by circumstances and in part by the weather. At least two hours a day, split up into four half-hour sessions or into a dozen ten-minute spells of freedom, is the smallest amount of exercise a Scottish Terrier should be expected to make do with. Exercise is essential for aiding the excretory organs, bowels, kidneys, etc., in their work, for oxygenizing the blood and for developing the muscles. Except for in-whelp bitches, part of it therefore should consist of really fast running about free in some enclosed place.

As already said, the Scot is a very adaptable person and will accommodate himself better than most dogs to prevailing conditions. If he has to live in a town flat he will adapt himself contentedly to the daily walk on a lead in the park or the streets, and be happy and none the worse provided the routine is kept up regularly and he has his freedom indoors. But when weather prevents a walk, such a dog must be given more energetic play indoors somehow. Our breed's sense of fun and playfulness, usually maintained right on into old age, is one of its greatest charms and is a big help when, for the good of his health, the dog will join in an energetic ball game up and down a corridor or other safe place, for a few minutes several times a day. Be warned over balls, however, only using the solid rubber sort specially sold for dogs, They must be big enough to make swallowing them impossible and should be never left lying about for the dog to chew. Tennis balls should never be used, nor should golf balls. The former are far too easy for the dog to tear apart, and one hears of too many cases of serious disorders, often ending fatally, resulting from dogs swallowing sections of rubber balls. The dangerous habit of encouraging a dog to play with stones should be ruled out too.

Country-dwelling dogs have better facilities for exercise, and in addition to the free gallops they should have either in a main yard, or a rough paddock or both, or around the garden if it is a spacious one with a dog-proof fence, a short walk on lead on the roads is desirable, partly for benefiting the dog's feet and partly because it gives added interest to his life and widens his outlook. Many owners have their dogs walked regularly on leads in all weathers, wet or fine. This is a sound enough principle provided every dog is *most thoroughly* dried on returning home wet. The best and quickest method for drying is to place the dog in a deep box full of dry clean sawdust, which may be kept in a position solely for this purpose. Rub the dust well into the coat all over with, special attention to the underbody and hindquarters, being watchful none gets into his eyes, and it is found the sawdust not only dries but cleans off any collected mud. Drying of the head and face can be completed with a chamois leather. The sawdust method is not suitable for dogs kept in the house, and for these a supply of chamois leathers reserved for the purpose are more absorbent than the average bath-towel. The main thing is to dry immediately every dog that has got wet. The drying of even three or four dogs after a wet or muddy walk may take longer than the walk itself, and if it is not going to be cheerfully undertaken far better cut out the walk that day. On days when walks are unavoidably curtailed, extra time and more vigour can well be devoted to the grooming, for brisk brushing stimulates the dog's circulation and makes him feel appreciated and companionable even though not enjoying his usual outing.

Every dog on a public highway should be on a lead. Loose dogs are a menace in town and country alike, both to motorists and to other dog-owners. It seems incredible that anyone caring for a dog sufficiently to want to own one at all should allow it to

(Sally Anne Thompson)
Ch. Gosmore Eilburn Admaration

Ch. Ortley Sandy

(Sally Anne Thompson)
Ch. Gosmore Eilburn Miss Hopeful

Ch. Niddbank Miss Blue Print

(Sally Anne Thompson)
Ch. Gaywyn Wicked Lady

Ch. Kennelgarth Viking *(centre)*. *Left:* his dam, Ch.
Kennelgarth Gleam. *Right:* his sire, Ch. Kennelgarth Eros

(Thorburn)

Ch. Medwal Wild Oats

Ch. Westpark Derriford Baffie

Ch. Glenview Guardsman

Ch. Con of Conett

roam the roads, as unfortunately many do; while dogs off leads at any time on a public highway, even though accompanied, are just as much a danger to all road-users. Besides risking the dog's own life it endangers that of human beings, for many a bad car smash has been caused by the driver endeavouring to avoid running over a dog and ending up by killing someone else.

It may be possible in some districts to let a couple or so terriers run loose on fields, commons or woodland, well away from roads and where it is known no rabbit snares or traps are set, but they should have been so trained from puppyhood that they obey commands and are under control all the time, and on returning to the road home should be led. There should be no sense of undue restriction in the dog's mind about being led; a well-brought-up dog looks upon the whole business as a a joyful proceeding and a real privilege, and is full of enthusiasm at the sight of his collar and lead being taken from its hook.

Actually, all dog-owners would be much better off if a law were passed making it a punishable offence for any dog to be loose outside its owners' property, other than those engaged at specified times on their legitimate jobs, such as hounds, gun-dogs, shepherd-dogs, and terriers employed in badger-digging or a rat-hunt. It would put an end to stray dogs and reduce much of the haphazard breeding of mongrels, thereby ultimately benefiting the breeders of pure stock. But let us hope no owner of that unique and wonderful thing a Scottish Terrier will ever allow himself or herself to be classed among the careless and the inconsiderate who own a dog and yet half the time don't know where it is because it is allowed out loose.

In hot weather exercising should be done in the early morning and the cool of the evening, and the dogs left resting in shaded places during the heat of the day. In winter exercise needs to be more brisk and frequent.

Training

There can be few things more irritating to either the owner or his friends than a totally undisciplined dog. The average Scottish Terrier, given a fair chance, has a genuine desire to please and is no happier for being untrained. Rather the reverse, for the gaining of well-deserved praise for his having obeyed even

D

the smallest commands makes him a very happy dog. With each lesson learnt, as he progresses along the paths of virtue and knowledge, he becomes increasingly easy to teach. A Scot gives his heart and devotion mainly to one person, usually the one who loves and understands him best, and will respond cheerfully to that persons' schooling, though in fresh hands he may at first appear stupid or obstinate. This philosophic breed, as has been said earlier, possesses an innate tendency towards good behaviour, being neither noisy, yapping, excitable or savage by nature. If a Scottie gets that way it is due to his owner's or trainer's influence. To know a persons' dogs is to get a pretty shrewd idea of that person's mentality, for most dogs, and Scots in particular, have the peculiar gift of reflecting their owner's personality.

Scottish Terriers are very tractable if understood. They can never be beaten or coerced into obedience. The best results, and by far the most lasting, are got by consistent kindness coupled with firmness, and unending patience. Patience is probably the quality most needed, for until the trainer fully understands the working of the dog's mind and gains its complete trust his temper may be sorely tried. Training in its simplest form should begin very early in a puppy's life. It is wise to accustom puppies even hardly out of the nest to names of their own. It is never too early to encourage this sense of identity in a puppy, and it pays later. But never repeat the call-name needlessly. Frequent reiteration of a dog's name makes him so sick of the sound of it that he eventually ceases to respond to it, knowing full well it has become meaningless. His name should in the first place be associated in his mind with reward in the shape of food. It takes but a few days for a puppy to learn his own name if this name is spoken every time he is given his meals, and thereafter during all his growing months the use of his name should be connected only with pleasant happenings such as being let out for a scamper, taken out on a lead or joining in a ball game. The same method of approach with food applies to all the early lessons. Gain his interest by means of tasty reward. It is a useful habit when going around the kennels among the young stock to have always in your pocket some bits of biscuit or some of the well-dried liver which will be alluded to in the chapter on Showing. Make in this way a regular practice of rewarding with a titbit the puppy which comes promptly when called by its name. But you *must* be consistent. Never call a puppy unless you do want it to come to you and are going to reward it immediately when it does. In fact all the way through the gradual education of a dog, it is essential to mean what you say to him.

Having established this early habit of attentiveness by dint of baits and rewards so that the puppy knows who he is and that to be called by name means responding quickly, begin gradually teaching him the meanings of other words.

In these days of so many organized classes for the obedience training of dogs, many useful tips may be picked up by attendance at such classes, but any wise owner will devise methods for himself whereby the elementary education of young dogs is part of the daily routine. If breeding dogs, whether for profit or pleasure or both, the necessity for giving as much thought to their temperaments and mental balance as is given to their physical well-being is clearly a serious responsibility. Breeders who neglect the mental and moral progress of their puppies are doing an injustice not only to the pups themselves but to the breed in general. Any kennel depends to some extent upon the sales of young stock to help pay its way, and reputations are as much made or marred by the behaviour and intelligence of the stock sold as by its external merits. Puppies and children are much alike in their early reactions. Development of character in both begins at a very early age, though it progresses more quickly in the dog, and good behaviour instincts can be cultivated by gentle and judicious discipline. Heredity naturally plays a part in the mental make-up of any animal, but subsequent training and environment can work wonders even with an unfavourable inheritance.

Never lose your temper with a dog. He will despise you for it, his trust in you is weakened, and his next response is likely to be all the slower in consequence. We are dealing with a creature of habit, and habits both good and bad are very easily formed when young, but the bad ones are not so easily cured. So begin as you mean to go on. It is unreasonable to let puppies jump up and paw at you while little, and then because they continue to do it when older (and with muddy feet) to get annoyed with them. It is ridiculous to say 'No' to a puppy one minute and then let him do the forbidden thing the next. The dog soon sums you up. If a person is variable, inconsistent and altogether unpredictable nobody is more quickly aware of it than the Scot. He will 'play up' in such hands, for it appeals greatly to his innate sense of humour to test his own strength of character against that of his owner.

In training, it is not so much what you say as the way you say it which means everything to the dog. Provided his trust and respect are won, the varying tone of your voice is most important to him, and he will quickly sense your pleasure or disapproval. Never shout at him; his hearing is far more acute than your own. Correction must be given at times, when just and necessary, but tone of voice is far more effective than a blow. The dog is very appreciative of praise and sensitive to scolding. In many cases the most perfect obedience can be attained by tones of voice alone. If and when forcible correction has to be applied, make it one smart smack with the hand, and one only, merely to let the dog know who is boss. Do not use a whip, stick, or rolled-up newspaper for dealing out such punishment, for the association of ideas will make the dog suspicious of these items for the rest of his life.

Training a youngster to be house-clean is not the difficult task it is sometimes set out to be. It merely calls for reasonable common sense and forethought on the trainer's part, and there are two main points to bear in mind. One is that it is necessary and natural for a puppy to relieve itself *immediately* after every meal. Consequently he should be watched while feeding and at the very moment he finishes his meal take him to the place where he is allowed to perform his natural functions. Tiny pups very quickly get used to going on a newspaper spread on the floor always in the same place. Older ones can be taken outdoors momentarily, and the moment they have done what is expected of them they should be suitably praised and brought in again. Many owners wisely accustom their young stock to a repeated phrase on these occasions, such as 'make haste', 'be quick', or 'get ready'. If used consistently it is amazing how soon the puppy recognizes the same word of command and understands its meaning, forming a habit which stands both owner and dog in good stead later on when you may want the dog to hurry over his necessary jobs in an appointed place at a given time. The other point to remember is that no puppy under six months can be expected to remain clean indoors all night. If not given the chance after midnight and again before six in the morning, suitable provision should be made for him to relieve himself during the night, and he must not be blamed when he does so.

Should a mistake occur in the house, never scold the offender *unless* he is caught actually in the act, otherwise he cannot possibly associate his offence with your displeasure. In any case, a disapproving tone of voice as you tell the puppy he was naughty and that this sort of thing is 'not done', is far more effective than any useless smacking.

Accustom all puppies to being handled quietly all over when on the grooming-table. Whether a house pet or a show dog in later life this habit stands him in good stead. He may have to be examined by a veterinary surgeon or a judge and to be restive and unmanageable is no help to anybody. Efforts must be made early in life to overcome any particular puppy's resentment to such handling, for to allow him once to get the upper hand is to lay up trouble for the future. It is a good plan to get strangers who visit the kennels to handle each puppy on a table, with yourself in close attendance. Especially accustom the puppies to having their mouths and teeth examined daily without protest.

Never fail to reward and praise the puppy which comes when called. Training in obedience can so easily fit in with the normal day's routine, though a very few minutes' special instruction now and then to each puppy separately is time well spent. Never attempt any special lesson when the puppy has just been fed or is sleepy, or if your own patience is exhausted. Be very sure the dog understands what is required of him, and be very patient yet consistently firm. To punish a puppy when he ultimately comes to you after defying the first call is the worst sort of foolishness, for he will take pains to stay out of your reach altogether next time. In a kennel of dogs disobedience is easy to overcome; if a defiant youngster fails to come when called, take the other dogs away with you, giving them titbits and lots of praise, leaving the defiant one where he was. Ignore him utterly. Some while later on you will find at the next call he comes at once. Usually in a kennel there are one or more adults of good moral example whose influence may be very helpful in training the youngsters, for dogs learn much more quickly from another of their kind than from humans.

Training to the lead is an essential part of every puppy's education, and is best commenced at about the age of four months. For the initial experience take a supply of tasty titbits and either a thin slip-cord or a light-weight soft collar and lead. Introduce both food and lead to the pup at the same time. The chief aim should be that the very sight of a lead becomes associated in the pup's mind with food, fun, and general lightheartedness. Reward him while first encircling his neck, and fix the collar or the slip so that there is room to insert one finger but it is not loose enough to pull over his ears. If he is inclined to chew or play with the lead at first don't discourage him, for he is getting to like it and that is what you want. Do not rush matters. Some Scots take to a lead like ducks to water, but those who do not need very patient handling. With the lead in your left hand and titbits in your right, bribe the puppy at first to come along a few steps after the food. Every short advance on his part must be instantly rewarded. Do not at first apply too much restraint; if he is the sort that plunges and rears like a restive horse give him lots of rein, even drop your end of the lead awhile and give him time to get used to the feel of the collar. The first lesson should be barely more than momentary. Increase its duration by degrees. With gentle persuasion and frequent practise on the same lines he will soon forget the strange feeling of something round his neck in his eagerness for the tasty rewards, and at that stage accustom him to keeping always at your left side. Another detail to watch is keeping the point of attachment between collar and lead either under the puppy's jaw or by the right side of his face: in other words never pull him from overhead with the collar dragging against his ears. Much harm can be done to the base of the ears and their ultimate carriage by this carelessness. Never on any account use harness for a Scot in place of collar and lead. These outfits have a harmful effect on the shoulders and fronts of growing puppies, and incidentally they only cause a dog to pull hard on his lead. If there is more than one puppy, living together, never leave a collar on any of them. Pups have a way of chewing each other's collars when at play, and I once had a serious case of near-strangulation due ro the teeth of one becoming jammed in the collar of another, revolving several times in its efforts to get loose, until the second pup's collar was like a tourniquet.

Some dogs have an inborn tendency to pull on the lead, which should be checked at the outset, once they have learnt to lead cheerfully. Otherwise it becomes a habit very difficult to cure in an older dog, a tiring one for all concerned, and detrimental to the dog's correct movement. At the first sign of pulling forward unduly, give the lead a short sharp jerk, using a word of reproof at the same time. Be consistent and stick to the same word. This jerk back may have to be repeated a few times, but it should not take long for the dog to realize how foolish it is to keep on pulling and inviting this sudden check. Another remedy for this habit is frequently and suddenly to reverse your direction, turning round and walking a few yards the opposite way. In training to lead, just as in feeding, try to stick to a routine by giving a few minutes' practise at the same time every day. If the initial stages have been made happy, as they should be, the dog will look forward to it as much as he does to his meal-times.

After learning to lead nicely, on a fairly slack lead and on the left side, every dog should be accustomed gradually to being tied up for short periods occasionally. Fix the lead (to something immovable, of course) and with the command 'Stay' leave him, for only a minute or so at first. If he chews the lead use a chain. It may save him a lot of heartbreak later on to learn to accept this position resignedly, and is of course essential practice for show dogs. The same applies to being boxed now and then. It is far kinder to accustom the youngsters to being shut in a travelling-box for a few moments periodically while still in the home circle than to risk subjecting them to the shock of it later without previous experience.

When a dog has reached an age of discretion, from about six months onwards, the chaining-up and the boxing are either of them invaluable aids towards good behaviour as regards house cleanliness. Dogs hate to soil their own sleeping-quarters, and if owners who have any trouble with those which are not clean indoors all night would give either method a trial they would soon achieve the desired result. Boxing is safer if the dog is alone in a room, the urgent necessity being to have him out first thing in the morning and very last thing at night. But when expected to accompany his owner and be a clean bedroom dog, chain him up for the night close to his own bed, from which position he will, by rattling his chain, rouse you to take him out in the morning rather than commit any offence. Times without number this method has saved from ruin a costly carpet in the house of a friend or in an hotel.

Training to develop good temperament throughout a kennel

of dogs should obviously include judicious discouragement of un-necessary barking. Prospective clients visiting a kennel take a dim view of being unable to hear themselves speak. Scots if sensibly raised seldom have any natural inclinations in this direction, but the habit may be acquired from a newcomer in their midst, or from ill-planned kennelling, or it may originate if a shy one crops up among the home-breds. Never retain a shy puppy in a kennel if you can avoid doing so, however externally beautiful it may be. Its influence can do incalculable harm to the mentality of the rest of the inmates. The instinctive diffidence and reserve of the breed in general must not be confused with actual shyness. The typical Scot does not gush over everybody he meets, and may permit himself a bark or two at the approach of strangers, as an assertion of his independence, but upon investigation and finding the strangers may be written off as harmless, he accepts their presence with cool politeness. A congenitally shy dog, on the other hand, will keep up a running commentary of short nervous barks at the sight and sound of every stranger coming to the place. If he is a coward as well he will run away and hide while barking. Such scaremongers are a menace, for the young stock imitate them too quickly. With dogs of normal intelligence the best method of discouraging barking at people is to make free use of the bits of rusk, liver, or biscuit which – as stated earlier – should be ready in your pocket. Link up in the dog's mind the idea of a tasty titbit coinciding with the arrival of strangers, and they will acquire the good habit of showing off brightly in front of visitors, their tails gay and no undue barking. When you invite visitors into your kennel-yard, make a point of handing a titbit to any dog that may bark and interrupt your conversation, for it cannot bark and swallow at the same time, and soon gets the notion that visitors to the place mean a pleasant interlude. It is very bad policy to show any anger with a persistently noisy one in such circumstances for then a dog will associate visitors with punish-ment and become more shy of them. In such cases pick the dog up quietly, talk to him reassuringly and put him away in his kennel, not forgetting to give him an extra biscuit or bit of liver.

Grooming

Every dog should be groomed thoroughly daily. Not only is it essential to cleanliness and consequently good health, it should be undertaken kindly, firmly and pleasantly so that the dog views it as one of his daily treats. Have a solid table or bench kept for the purpose, of a convenient height for the owner to work on the dog without incurring backache. Be supplied with steel combs, both coarse and fine, a stiff-bristled brush, scissors and a coarse carpenter's file.

Some days the grooming may be merely a brief combing through with coarse comb, followed by a few moments' brisk brushing. If the coat is thus tended daily no tangles should form around the underparts of each leg, but if they ever do, cut the matted hair carefully away with scissors rather than torture the dog by trying to tease out mats with a comb. Once a week at the very least grooming should constitute a complete overhaul of every detail. In addition to the preliminary brushing and combing, this includes the careful examination of eyes, ears, teeth, feet and anal glands. For simple eye and ear remedies refer to Chapter 14 If the dogs have been properly fed on dry foods and crisp rusks, and had their fair chance of gnawing big marrow-bones, there should be nothing wrong with their teeth until extreme old age.

It is extremely important to keep the feet in good condition. Unless the dogs are regularly walked on hard roads, many of them will grow their toenails too long. Overlong nails, besides being unsightly, have a very adverse effect on the front, shoulders and action of the dog. In cases where dew-claws have been left on, these particularly need watching to prevent them ever becoming overgrown, as they may get torn or broken, or curl right round until pressing into the flesh and so set up inflammation.

When the nails have been well looked after and kept short from puppyhood, the maintenance of a well-trimmed foot should be easy. It is well to accustom every puppy to the use of the file on each claw, and is a job more comfortably done by sitting in a chair with the pup on your lap, and with the left arm cosily round him grasp each separate claw very firmly between thumb and finger of the left hand. With the right hand, rub the coarse file smoothly up and down against the point of the claw. The puppy soon loses all sense of alarm at the unusual feeling if the grip of its toe in your left hand remains very firm, and it is a perfectly painless proceeding, preferable to using nail-clippers. In cases of neglect, or if for any reason road walks have been curtailed, or while a bitch has been nursing puppies, sometimes the nails are found too long to wear down quickly enough with a file, so the nail-clippers have to be resorted to. But the greatest care should be taken to avoid removing more than a tiny bit at a time. Better to take longer over the task and wear away a little each day than to risk cutting into the quick of the nail, for once that excruciating pain in inflicted the same dog will never stand for the chance of a repetition and becomes difficult to handle.

The growth of the nails varies very much with individuals, and it is found that the dogs with the best feet – round, firm and thickly padded – seldom require much attention of this sort. Even these feet, however, can deteriorate if the dog is only exercised on grass.

Too many dogs are often suspected of having worms if they are seen rubbing themselves along the ground in a sitting position. This is usually due to the glands surrounding the anus becoming congested. In a state of Nature, the dog's evacuations are harder, so that the passing of each motion keeps the anal glands in order. But under civilized conditions slight discomfort often arises, and unless dealt with promptly and regularly may lead to the forming of an abcess. It should be part of the thorough examination to make sure the dog is absolutely clean under the tail and around the anus, and whether he needs it or not the anal glands should be occasionally squeezed out. This is a simple job which takes but a moment to do during the grooming session, and either your veterinary surgeon or a fellow breeder of experience will demonstrate exactly how it is done.

In the ordinary way, and if grooming has been systematically and thoroughly carried out, bathing a Scot is not necessary or desirable, for it softens the coat texture and may render the dog liable to chill. If it ever has to be undertaken, use only a soap or shampoo specially prepared for dogs, and make very sure of the subsequent thorough drying, followed by brisk exercise to warm the dog up before being kennelled.

One does not anticipate fleas, lice, ticks, or other intruders in the coat of a well-groomed dog, but since these unwanted guests are sometimes passed on from other animals or picked up at a show it is a sound practice to finish off by dusting a little safe insect powder into the coat. For young puppies use a home-prepared dusting powder of half pyrethrum and half sulphur, because it is safer than any of the advertised brands should some inadvertently get into their eyes.

7

Breeding

Theoretical

The qualities desirable in those who set out to breed Scottish Terriers successfully are patience, perseverance, tireless energy, undying enthusiasm, a real love of the breed and the optimistic temperament of never-ending hope. It is neither a matter of haphazard luck nor of scientific accuracy. There is no short cut to success. If a breeder has luck the occupation may prove profitable as well as pleasurable, but after all luck is mainly skill and good management. To the true breeder profit is welcome if it results, but largely because it is regarded as proof of success.

The true breeder aims high. He is out to breed the best possible; dogs which are intelligent and healthy, a credit to their ancestry and their breeder, and which can win in the keenest competition. He has a goal in view, the ultimate production of the perfect Scottish Terrier, and to this end all his efforts will be directed. He rates the welfare of the breed as a whole more highly than his own personal gain, therefore is keenly alive to a sense of responsibility.

First and foremost, the aim in breeding should be for dogs with brains, stamina, and self-confidence: for of what use is the beautiful fool or the weakling. On this basis, breed to breed. This means working on a prearranged plan, and implies forethought, arranging each mating with the reasonable expectation that the progeny will not only be an improvement on their parents but may serve to further advance this improvement in subsequent generations.

It is in inbreeding that skill in breeding especially lies. Any idiot can mate two closely related animals, but it is the skilled breeder who knows how and when to inbreed. The breeder must know and thoroughly understand the two units he is mating. Seeing an animal and noting its merits or defects is not enough. He must know whence these came, and this necessitates a knowledge of ancestry. Some inbreed on paper. But inbreeding is very much a matter of the individuals used. Pedigree is of great importance; the very fact that one is inbreeding is a matter of pedigree on paper, but the relative merits and demerits of the animals used become of more importance than when one is mating distantly related animals. For breeding purposes an animal has two main factors, its own conformation and its pedigree. Pedigree is a dormant part of an animal which comes into play when that animal is called upon to reproduce its kind. The names in a pedigree are merely cyphers, indicating certain groupings of features and certain sources of blood, and unless the breeder can translate what these cyphers stand for the pedigree is meaningless to him. Novice breeders would be well advised to acquire all possible information about the ancestry of the stock with which they propose to start breeding, for it is only in this way the potentialities of their stock can be assessed and the value of pedigree appreciated.

Until an animal is bred from we cannot be certain which of its inherited qualities it may transmit to its progeny, but with consanguineous matings the element of uncertainty is greatly reduced. Consanguinity of blood implies either inbreeding or linebreeding. the same results may be obtained by both methods, but line-breeding is a longer way round to reach the same destination. By inbreeding is usually meant a close-up repetition to a pedigree of the same individuals, such as the mating of sire to daughter, or a dam to her son, or a brother and sister. These are the closest forms possible, but there are many alternative variations. Line-breeding implies a repetition of the same blood in a pedigree, but not necessarily through the same individuals. Whichever one calls it, line-breeding or inbreeding, it is a system practised to secure uniformity of essential characters. Several examples can be studied among the pedigrees set out in Chapter 2. For instance, Ch. Albourne Admiration was the result of linebreeding to the male blood; Ch. Albourne Barty showed linebreeding both to the male blood and to the Family.

There is an unreasonable prejudice in some lay minds against any form of inbreeding. Criticism usually comes from the one-pet-dog owner, who is all too ready to attach blame to the fact that his dog is too 'highly bred' as he calls it, when the wretched animal is the victim of some disorder plainly due to the owner's mismanagement. There was at one time widespread belief that in-breeding of itself could cause lack of vitality, sterility and the appearance of abnormalities. There is absolutely no foundation for such belief. Inbreeding of itself can create no traits or charac-teristics which are not already present in the stock inbred to. If defects of any kind result from inbreeding it is not the fault of the system but of the breeder who may have insufficient know-ledge of the material he is using and selects unsuitable stock for the purpose. Inbreeding intensifies the points and characteristics, *both good and bad*, which are already present in the blood. Therein lies its chief danger in the hands of the inexperienced, for faults as well as virtues are equally intensified. You can inbreed defects as well as points of merit, just as you can inbreed health, stamina and the right temperament as well as disease or deformities. In-breeding is a system which must be followed on very careful and scientific lines. If attempted, it should be done with animals markedly free from defects either mental or physical, and whose forbears for many generations were likewise free from taint. Un-desirable qualities can lie dormant for six or seven generations, or maybe longer, and then reappear to upset the finest calcula-tions. Mental soundness is more important than all else. It can be bred for just as much as any physical feature, and evidence of any weakness in mind or nerves shows mistaken breeding. The temptation to breed from good-looking but nervous animals is great, in the hope of their transmitting their good looks, but it is a temptation that should be resisted at all costs.

In our breed it is difficult to avoid line-breeding to male lines. Past results have proved, however, that line-breeding to a Family, or female line has met with greater success. Some owners are inclined to attach too much importance to the influence of the sire. They mate indifferent bitches to an outstanding sire in the belief that he will transmit his characteristics to the offspring. The dog that can do this is described as prepotent. But many a dog with an impressive show record and great individual merit does not possess this property. And prepotency is not the property of sires only; dams may be just as prepotent. An animal may be prepotent for one characteristic and not for others. Ch. Heather Necessity, for instance, was strongly prepotent for good tempera-ment apart from all else. Albourne Annie Laurie was prepotent for many external virtues, particularly correct breed type. Prepotency usually depends on the purity of the animals mated; in other words, those which have been constructively line-bred for many generations are liable to be more prepotent than those of indiscriminate breeding.

Normally it is an ambition of every breeder worthy the name to build up a strain of his own. A strain can only be described as such when the same blood has been in one ownership for many generations. It is the possession of a family of animals carrying certain distinguishing family characteristics while yet conforming to breed type. It has been said that in every animal four types may be represented – the individual type (since no two animals are ever identical in every detail), the family type, the strain type, and the breed type. In the early days of our breed's show history, when there were many more real breeders and far fewer exhibitors, it used to be quite easy to recognize for instance an Ornsay, a Merlewood, or an Ems type of dog at a glance, from the fact that each bore the stamp of the strains from which they were produced. They had a strain type. Just because every dog in a given kennel carries the same registered prefix before its name is no reason for presupposing that kennel has a strain of its own. To ascertain whether it has or not requires a thorough probing into the pedigrees for seven or eight generations.

In establishing a kennel, and eventually a strain, the greatest emphasis should be placed on the bitches selected. The strength of a kennel lies in its bitches, therefore too much care and consideration can hardly be given to the initial choice of the bitches with which it is hoped to found a successful kennel. Individual merit and ancestry are the two main considerations. The better the average of good bitches in a kennel, the better the average of the puppies bred. Man has three opportunities of using his influence in the propagation of a breed: in the selection of a sire, the selection of a dam, and the selection of the offspring. Of these the first selection usually made is that of the dam. It is well if one can be acquired from an established strain of good producers, preferably tracing in tail-female descent from one of the recorded Families. In addition to that the principal requirement is that she conforms in general appearance to the true build of the breed, that she is not just a mixture of points but is essentially a Scottish Terrier with the unique conformation distinguishing it from any other breed; plus a good temperament.

There must be no hurry in building up a strain. The progress made should be slow and sure. There will be setbacks of course, but breeding dogs is no job for the fainthearted. Breed for the improvement of one feature at a time. Make it a rule that in all matings the animals used have that feature strongly emphasized in their blood. By pursuing this course for three or four generations the desired feature becomes sufficiently fixed to enable the breeder to risk something in the next selection of a mate in order to obtain some other feature. There is a theory on inbreeding which was held by the late John A. Doyle. He was a great authority and author of American history, a Master of Harriers, a most successful breeder of racehorses and Fox-Terriers and served for many years on the Kennel Club Committee. His theory was that the strain inbred to should appear either in the 1st and 4th quarters, or in the 2nd and 3rd quarters of the pedigree, but never in the 1st and 3rd, or 2nd and 4th. There is more in this than may at first appear, since to inbreed 1st and 4th, or 2nd and 3rd, means one has got to possess decent stock of *both* sexes with which to do the inbreeding.

To anyone wishing to learn more about the genetics of dog-breeding, the principles governing canine inheritance and how they may be applied, I strongly recommend Dr. Fitch Daglish's book *The Dog Breeder's Manual*.

Selecting the right stud dog to suit a bitch is often the breeder's biggest headache. There are four main factors to keep in mind: his type, his temperament, his pedigree and his points. In general type and conformation he should resemble the bitch as much as possible. Mating sharp contrasts is to invite failure. His temperament and personality play a big part; all the greatest sires in the breed have possessed assertive and dominating personalities. He should look essentially masculine and display self-confidence under all circumstances. It is most desirable to have seen the dog at home as well as in the show-ring. His pedigree should supply a repetition of some of the best blood in the pedigree of the bitch, but the greatest stress should be laid upon the dam of the sire selected and the bitch blood throughout his pedigree. The dog's dam and her ancestors will have more influence over the stock he may sire than his paternal antecedents. This has been proved conclusively in our breed. Consequently it is most desirable to know all that can be learnt about the dam of the stud dog to be used. Many people delude themselves into thinking that the sire selected will contribute all his virtues and none of his failings and will correct any faults in the bitch. A vain hope. Another mistake frequently made is rushing to use the latest champion merely because he is a champion. On pedigree, type and temperament he may be absolutely unsuited. He may even be a chance-bred good-looker, produced more or less unexpectedly from a poor stamp of bitch. They do happen. But avoid using a stud dog whose bitch blood is of no account. The light-boned quality dog which gives the impression he would have made a better bitch is seldom a success at stud. One must look for substance, bone and character, and remember that most great sires, whatever the breed of animal, possess a look of distinction about the head.

The aim should be to raise the general average in a kennel. This cannot be done all at once by using the latest senational winners as sires, regardless of their suitability. The higher the average of good bitches kept in the kennel the greater is the likelihood of one day breeding the outstanding show dog. Stud dogs should therefore be selected as a means towards this desired end, that of a gradual but sure improvement in the average of the kennel. Much patient perseverance and tenacity of purpose is called for, and from every litter bred the best bitch puppy should be retained for future breeding progress until it is proved conclusively that she does not possess one single feature showing an improvement upon her dam. It is usually tempting providence to part with the best bitch of a litter, until one has something better from another litter.

Practical (for the Novice)

In the choice of the foundation bitches and in strict attention to detail lie the secrets of success (if there be any) in the breeding of Scottish Terriers. Unless you have suitable accommodation for rearing puppies and are prepared to spend both time and money on providing the best of care and food, 'twere better to leave dog-breeding to others. However good the initial stock may be, it will benefit nobody unless properly looked after. At the outset it is well to ascertain from whence regular supplies of good lean meat can be obtained. Meat is the dog's natural diet, and for

breeding stock it is absolutely essential. Bitches from which one
intends to breed must be kept in good fettle by a plentiful supply
of meat and plenty of exercise.

The best way to make a start is with one or two well-bred
bitches which are proved breeders. An axiom which should be
much more rigidly observed is – 'No animal is well bred unless
it is good in itself'. For nothing hinders improvement of stock so
much as rating pedigree of higher importance than the individual. A very large proportion of pedigree stock is not good in
itself, and is bred from because of its ancestry, the failings of which
it has inherited rather than the virtues. These failings will undoubtedly repeat themselves sooner or later. Such inferior specimens may occasionally breed good-looking progeny, but these in
their turn will be unreliable breeding material. So the choice of
brood bitch should rest both on appearance and pedigree. The
chance-bred good-looker is as valueless for breeding as is the
mediocre specimen with a mile-long pedigree full of champions.

By a proved breeder is meant one of maybe two to four years
of age which has whelped easily one or more litters and mothered
her pups well. Such a bitch, if sound and from a good strain, will
cost more to buy than an unproved younger one, but the extra
outlay is usually worth while. Just occasionally such a bitch may
be acquired on breeding terms; an arrangement by which the
lender has a claim on some of the pups in lieu of payment for the
bitch. It is an inexpensive way to begin, but has its drawbacks
since the borrower usually comes off with the second best from a
litter. The original owner is fully justified in demanding first pick
of the puppies, and in proportion to the value of the bitch loaned
he may require similar recompense from several litters bred,
before the contract is fulfilled. Thus a few years may elapse before
the borrower finds himself in a position to retain the best bitch
puppy, which is what he wants if progress is to be made, and it
is possible, though not necessarily so, that the bitch herself may
by that time have passed her best producing years. Breeding terms
vary a lot, and may be anything the two contracting parties agree
to, but should any plan of this sort be entertained, do be warned
and have every detail of the agreement, as well as every possible
contingency, in writing, signed by both parties, and preferably
also registered at the Kennel Club. Even the best of friends have

been known to fall out by depending on each other's none too good memories over such arrangements.

Some people prefer to make a start by buying a bitch puppy and having the fun of raising and training it with the intention of breeding from it in due course. If the puppy be purchased at about eight weeks old, this is perhaps the least costly method, but it is nothing but a gamble at the best of times. It is unlikely a breeder will sell you the best bitch puppy of a litter, except at a prohibitive price, and if you are inexperienced the puppy may not thrive as it should. It also means more than a year before you get results. Another alternative is to buy a maiden bitch of around a year old. In this case you do see what you are getting, but if she is worth while both on looks and pedigree she will be pretty costly, and again one is taking a chance for she may prove difficult to mate, or a non-breeder, or, if she breeds, a poor whelper.

Whichever age you decide upon, it is a wise policy to put your money into one really good bitch rather than spread the same amount over two or three indifferent specimens, however impressive their pedigrees may be. If two or more can be afforded at the outset it is quite a good idea to let one of them be a young bitch puppy, because though it may or may not prove an additional string to your bow for breeding with later on, you will be gaining experience over puppy rearing which stands you in good stead when other litters come along.

In your selection avoid the shy or quarrelsome bitch. It is usually the bitch that mixes peaceably with others of her own sex which makes the best mother. Look for body properties before head points, more particularly bone, ribs that are both wide and deep and well carried back, a muscular loin, and strong well-made quarters before all else. Don't let it worry you if ears, eyes, or front are not of the best, or if back and tail are a shade longer than the show-ring demands, for the body and hindquarter essentials mentioned first are of infinitely more importance in a brood bitch.

Bitches usually come in season for the first time between seven and ten months of age, but that varies with individuals, some starting as early as six months, and others not until well over a year. As a rule it is unwise to mate a bitch at her first heat, unless this does not occur until she is at least fourteen months old. Even then one should be sure she is well up to size, and in hard muscular condition, neither too fat nor too thin. Breeding checks further growth on her part, and to use a bitch younger than this is to impose an unfair strain on her own development and that of the pups. Actually Scots in the main are not fully matured until eighteen months of age; some take even longer to come to their best. Do not, however, delay breeding from a maiden bitch much later than two years of age. After three years old there is considerable risk over whelping a first litter.

Before she is due in season, make sure the bitch to be bred from is clean inside and out. This implies freedom from worms and a clean healthy skin. The period or heat starts with a swelling of the vulva and a slight discharge. This will become blood-coloured and usually lasts for about ten days. The best time for mating is when the colour has died away leaving the bitch still swollen and a little damp; approximately from the tenth to the fourteenth day from the time she commenced colouring. There are variations, so the bitch must be carefully examined every morning to ascertain what stage she has reached in her season.

It is imperative to book a service well in advance for the stud dog you intend using. Tell the dog's owner about when you expect the bitch to come on heat, and he will if possible reserve the dog for near that date. Some popular sires are so fully booked up you may not always get the dog you want, so be prepared with a second choice in mind. If sending or taking the bitch to leave for some days at the kennels of the stud dog, send her while she is still colouring, for this guides the stud's owner as to the best time for mating. If taking her personally for her mating the same day, the remarks above may help you to pick on the right day, and you should plan to arrive at the kennels fully a couple of hours before the mating. With an old experienced bitch it is not so important, but with a young maiden it is essential to give her time to rest awhile after a journey, and before introducing her to the dog she should be given the chance to empty both bowels and bladder. After the mating is effected, another quiet rest of at least an hour is important for the bitch before her return journey. Pay the stud fee at the time of mating, and if the bitch has spent several days at the kennels enquire whether any charge is made in addition to cover her cost of keep. A stud fee is paid for the service of the dog, irrespective of whether the bitch proves in whelp or not. In most cases if she misses, another service is given free at her next season, but it is well to have a clear understanding on this point beforehand.

If you send a bitch by rail for her stud visit, use a roomy, well-ventilated and safe travelling-box, one which has a sensible door or lid and fastenings, and a rainproof top. Not a kind of 'Heath Robinson' contraption thrown together at the last minute, with slats or wire netting nailed down and causing infinite annoyance on arrival. Put a collar on her, but not a lead, and in addition to the clearly written address on the label, state her kennel name.

When the bitch returns home after mating, keep her fairly quiet for a couple of days. If the mating has been successful she usually goes off heat quickly, but some bitches can remain attractive to the male dog and in a condition to be mated for as long as a week after the first service, so watch her carefully. For the first five weeks of her pregnancy she can enjoy her normal routine; good meat feeding and regular exercise of the amounts to which she has been accustomed. You don't have to mollycoddle her, but certainly any strenuous exertion like chasing a ball, gambolling roughly with her kennel-mates, going up and down a flight of stairs or jumping off heights should be ruled out of her curriculum.

The period of gestation is sixty-three days, but Scots usually whelp a few days under this time, though now and again exceptions are met with which go over the time. Your veterinary surgeon can say, by feeling the bitch's abdomen at a stage between the twenty-first and twenty-eighth day after mating, whether she is in whelp. Once this is established, her feeding should be gently increased from her fifth week onwards. This is best done by an additional feed of lean meat at midday, rather than overload her stomach by increasing the amount at supper-time. Cod-liver oil, or halibut-oil, if not part of her normal diet, should be added to her food all through her pregnancy, as also calcium-phosphate or calcium-lactate which help to supply the puppies with bone-forming material. Be very sure that she always has access to plenty of clean drinking-water, and if she is in whelp in wintry weather and lives in an outside building, have the chill taken off the water before she drinks.

For quite a fortnight before the litter is expected the bitch should be accustomed to sleeping in the box in which she is to whelp. It is most unsettling to any bitch, especially one whelping for the first time, to be given new sleeping quarters at the last moment. They are full of notions at such times, and most of them prefer to have their pups in the box they know and are used to, provided it is in a suitably quiet secluded corner and in semi-darkness. So get her used to the properly planned whelping-box in good time; if introduced to it too late she may do herself serious injury trying to escape from the unfamiliar surroundings. Some bitches at the last moment, when whelping is imminent, have a strong urge to return to Nature by seeking seclusion in some quite inaccessible place, such as underneath a garden hut where nobody can reach her, and no amount of persuasion will get her out. So as the time draws near it is important to keep a watch on her and know just where she is.

The happiest existence for an in-whelp bitch is to be allowed the freedom of house and garden and be able to roam in and out of her own quarters at will, but the daily walk on a lead should be continued right on till whelping time or just as long as she is interested and willing to go. About three days before her full date, give the bitch a dessertspoonful of olive oil or liquid paraffin. This can be added to her evening meal and the taste will not be noticed. Also for these last few days feed her more sparingly; continue with three feeds per day, but make the morning one a drink of some milky food, and reduce the bulk of the evening feed somewhat.

The chief points about a suitable whelping-place are warmth, privacy, quiet, and a draughtproof whelping-box of adequate dimensions. The temperature in the room or building should be kept at a steady sixty-five degrees Fahrenheit, never less. One of the most important things in rearing good puppies is that they should be born in sufficiently warm quarters. More newly born puppies are lost from lack of warmth at birth than from any other cause. They come from a very warm place and deserve the very warmest possible welcome into this world. Whatever the time of year it is almost impossible for their place of birth to be too warm, and even in midsummer arrangements should be made for arti-ficial heat, since bitches most often whelp at night or in the early hours of the morning and there are very few summer nights when the atmosphere is warm enough for pups to be born into it.

Puppies born in a heated temperature start life advantageously; they dry off more quickly and so receive no chill. In actual practice it is found puppies born thus are twice as strong after the first day as any born into even a medium temperature. This point cannot be emphasized too strongly and needs to be printed in heavy capital letters – WARMTH FOR NEWBORN PUPPIES. The very old and the very young must have warmth or they perish, and this applies to dogs just as much as to humans. It is therefore best to instal an infra-red lamp for newly born and quite young puppies. A dull Emitter bulb made by Phillips, similar to that used by pig breeders, is the best type to get, and if this is used it must never on any account be hung nearer than three-and-a-half feet above the whelping box. The best type for whelping is a box with access for the bitch at one end only. It must be large enough for her to be able to turn round freely and lie at full length with her puppies. Twenty-six by twenty-two inches suits most Scots. The box must be raised a couple of inches from the floor, which is high enough to avoid floor draughts yet low enough for the bitch to get in and out without difficulty. It should be constructed of well-fitting boards or of plywood and be free from cracks and crevices.

Across the entrance fix a low but removable ledge not more than two inches in depth, just to keep the bedding in. After the bitch has whelped, this ledge should be replaced by a four-inch board, with a smooth edge, over which she can by that time jump easily. This prevents the pups from being dragged or pushed out of bed, as often happens when they are hanging tightly on the teats.

The box must be open at the top for the rays of warmth from the lamp, but a wise precaution is to arrange that a portion of the open top is roofed so that the bitch herself can lie under the roofed portion when she feels too hot. The pups too will some-times seek shade from the lamp's rays in the same way, but for, the most part they thrive remarkably under the steady warmth of the lamp, maintained equably night and day.

For bedding in the whelping-box several layers of dry news-paper, with perhaps a small square of old blanket added, is as good as anything. Whatever is supplied the bitch will tear it all to shreds when whelping time approaches, and clean newspaper can be easily and frequently replaced as it becomes soiled.

This digging up and tearing at her bed is one of the signs that whelping is fairly imminent, as also is the fact that the bitch may refuse her food, and may also vomit. Leave her undisturbed at this stage and try to ensure that all is quiet in the near vicinity, the other dogs prevented from having noisy games, etc. The bitch may quite likely do her bed-making stunt a whole day or more before whelping actually starts, so take a look at her every few hours to note if she has begun to strain. When her labour-pains really begin she will pant a lot, breathe quickly, and show every sign of restlessness. Sometimes the first puppy is born within a few minutes of the onset of labour pains, but more often an hour to an hour and a half will elapse, the bitch alternating between bouts of vigorous straining and spells of rest in between to gather her strength. If no puppy has been born when the bitch has been in labour for three hours, then you must call in your veterinary surgeon for his advice. This is most important, and is the reason why you have to keep an eye on the bitch beforehand to know exactly when her labour pains started. It is presumed you will be on the books, so to speak, of a qualified veterinary surgeon, and it is always wise to let him know in advance when you have a bitch due to whelp in case you have to contact him in a hurry. What so very often happens is that the first puppy may either be extra large or may be wrongly presented, and so hold up the birth of the rest of the litter. Your veterinary surgeon can deal with this situation provided you have sought his advice in time, and most probably the remainder of the litter will then be born naturally. If you leave the bitch in labour too long without expert attention you may lose the whole litter and the bitch as well. It sometimes happens that the pups are all overbig and it would be a mechanical impossibility for the bitch to pass them through the pelvic arch, in which case a Caesarean operation is called for. The prevalence of these operations in recent years in our breed is greatly to be deplored, but when conditions are abnormal we must feel thankful that the advance of science and canine surgery makes it possible to save a bitch a lot of unnecessary suffering as can be caused by the use of forceps. On the whole, however, veterinary advice is not in favour of an operation if it can be avoided, so put your whole trust in your vet and follow his advice. If the pregnant bitch has been sensibly fed and thoroughly well exercised all along, the odds are very much in favour of her whelping naturally and easily. If a Caesarean operation has to be resorted to, it need not effect the bitch's value for subsequent breeding. Many that have undergone the operation once have whelped their next litters without assistance.

In a normal whelping the first thing you should notice is the protrusion from the bitch's vulva of the membraneous sac in which each puppy is enclosed. This means the first pup is well on its way, if progress is normal, but should this membrane recede again and the bitch has already been labouring for two hours, send at once for veterinary assistance. When the pup is born in the normal way, the bitch ruptures the enclosing membrane containing the pup, cleans up all the fluid that comes with it, and bites through the umbilical cord which attaches the puppy to the afterbirth, ending by consuming the afterbirth. She then licks the puppy vigorously and probably quite roughly, inducing it to breathe and emit its first cry, and the normally robust pup finds its way to a nipple and starts on its first feed. The bitch then rests quietly for possibly half an our or so, until the next labour pains indicate the arrival of the next puppy. Sometimes only ten minutes or less elapse between the pups, and one hears of bitches whelping a litter of eight pups in under two hours. But again, if there is undue delay of three hours or more after the first pup and it is obvious there are more to come, seek expert aid. The same process is repeated over each birth until all the litter is whelped, when the bitch settles down contentedly with her family. Many owners nowadays take the precaution of having a pregnant bitch X-rayed just a week before she is due. This is a sound plan, because the X-ray plate will show the number and the positions of the pups and enables your veterinary surgeon to know in advance what contingencies may arise. If everything is going along as described, you should leave the mother severely alone to get on with her job. It is best for only one person, the one to whom she is most accustomed and in whom she has confidence, to be in attendance on such occasions, and though there is with a normal whelping absolutely nothing for you to do except keep quiet, it is well to maintain an unobtrusive watch on proceedings in case of trouble arising. Sometimes a pup may appear to be stuck half-way out of the vulva if the bitch has been straining for some time and is unable to expel it; and this is probably the only occasion on which amateur aid may be given without doing any harm. Take a piece of towelling with which to grasp the protruding half of the pup, and exert slight but firm pressure to pull it out, but it is very important the pulling motion should only be applied while the bitch strains, so that her effort and yours coincide. Such pups usually come hind-feet first, and unless you are very quick ripping the membrane and severing the naval cord it will probably suffocate. The normal presentation is nose and forefeet first.

After the whole litter is born and the bitch resting, she and they are best left absolutely undisturbed for twenty-four hours. Do not imagine the bitch requires feeding immediately after such an ordeal. She is much better without it, and the first food offered to her after twenty-four hours should be nothing but a drop of warm milk or water and glucose. Resist the temptation to examine the pups on the first day. The less they are handled the better, for many a bitch is unnecessarily disturbed and agitated because of human curiosity. Time enough to discover the sexes of the pups on the second day, and if you prefer to remove their dew-claws this must be done at three or four days old, no later. Some breeders take them off, some don't; it is a matter of preference. It is a very simple job at that age; merely cut the offending claw off close to the foreleg with a pair of sharp surgical scissors, and dab the wound with an antiseptic. If much bleeding occurs the dam soon sees to it and they heal up within an hour or two.

To remove the soiled bedding, just take the first layer of newspaper away. If there is a dead puppy take this away with the paper, but be careful that the bitch does not notice – otherwise leave it till she goes out to relieve herself. Later on, the best covering for the bottom of the box is a section of stiff carpet, cut to fit the box exactly. There is nothing better for providing a firm resistance for the puppies' feet as they wriggle and squirm towards the dam. Sacking is sometimes used, tacked down firmly, but this is not to be recommended as the bitch may decide to uproot the whole thing, the tacks are a danger, and a puppy may get smothered under the loosened material. Stiff carpet is best, and have more than one piece cut to fit in readiness, so that it can be changed over and scrubbed. Never put any loosely woven material in with young pups. The cover provided for the rubber hot-water bottle should be of the harsh type of coarse flannel or blanket which does not catch into loops. Serious harm can be done to the tiny limbs and feet of the pups by their claws becoming entangled in unsuitable bedding material, and many a pup is lain on and squashed by the dam as a result.

For the first three days the nursing bitch must be fed solely on milky foods, and sparingly at that. A very small feed every four hours is best, and you can make it more interesting for her by alternating between thin oatmeal gruel, warm milk sweetened with honey, and such patent invalid or puppy foods as Benger's, Robinson's Groats, or Farex. If all is well after the third day, she can be gradually got back on to some good meat broth poured over wholemeal rusks, a small amount of white fish or some well-cooked rabbit. From then onwards she can resume her normal diet with additions. It is best to continue with four feeds a day as long as she is nursing puppies, and the additional meals should be on the liquid side for the first three weeks, in the form of good broth on wholemeal rusks and one of the milky feeds. She needs plenty of good nourishment, for the pups make increasing demands upon her every day. Continue with her cod-liver oil and the calcium.

The state of the dam's bowels must be watched. Her motions are fairly loose just after whelping, but if they become excessively so feed her a little well-boiled rice, or some arrowroot, with her milky meal. On the other hand if she is too costive, correct that by increasing the oatmeal or groats food.

At first the bitch will be very unwilling to come out of the box at all, but she should be gently yet firmly made to do so for a few moments, long enough to empty her bladder after the first twenty-four hours. Try to induce her to leave the pups for a moment each day, by supplying a fresh hot-water bottle and arranging the pups round it where they can feel the warmth; she will soon realize you mean no harm to her family if you offer her a warm drink of milk the while, and then take her outside for a moment. Go with her, so that she entertains no suspicion of what you may be doing to the litter in her absence. In fact, in every way while tending a nursing bitch do everything to keep her mind at rest, for any anxiety on her part can adversely affect her milk flow. For this reason too, you will be wise to forbid all strangers or visitors a glimpse of the new litter until they are quite a week old. When such times comes as admiring onlookers can be admitted, make it a rule that nobody handles or picks up a puppy

except yourself. The touch of a strange hand on a puppy is per-
ceived at once by the keen nose of the dam, who may visit her
resentment on the puppy itself; while should some clumsy
individual let one of your best pups fall you have only yourself
to thank. So take no chances.

In feeding a nursing mother, and later the puppies during
weaning, remember the great food value of honey. Add a teaspoonful to each milky feed. Suggested daily diet for bitch nursing
puppies, from the third day after whelping until pups are four
and a half weeks old:

> 8 a.m. Vary between raw egg and warm milk, with honey.
> Benger's food, with honey or glucose.
> Robinson's groats and milk, with honey or glucose.
> Oatmeal porridge and milk with honey or glucose.
> Farex (or similar) with milk.
>
> 12 noon. Raw lean meat chopped small, with half teaspoonful
> of cod-liver oil.
>
> 4 p.m. Some warm broth poured over brown rusks, or
> shredded wheat or similar wholemeal cereal, with
> calcium powder added.
>
> 8 p.m. Normal main meal of cooked meat, sometimes with
> rusks or good biscuit meal added.

If you add to this routine the very late or midnight drink of warm
milk, all the better.

Never be foolish enough to give a bone to a bitch with pups.
Jealousy and a bitten or dead pup will result, besides which it
tends to dry off her milk secretion. Some bitches need more help
with milk-producing foods than others, depending upon their
own milk secretions. Sometimes the dam's supply may have been
conditioned for a large litter from which only one or two survive,
in which case she may have too generous a flow of milk and you
must reduce her liquid feeds and give more meat. If on the other
hand she does not seem to secrete enough milk to satisfy the
demands of the youngsters, be more lavish with the eggs, milk
and honey, also good broth, and make very sure the bitch is
having enough daily exercise. She should not be dragged for a
walk against her will, but as soon as she will leave the pups wil-
ingly for a few moments, try to increase her time away from them
a little each day, and by the time they are three weeks old,

mother's absence for an hour will do no harm provided you have left them all cosily huddled round a hot-water bottle. Too much confinement for long periods with her growing litter is bad for her milk flow, and may easily cause her to lose interest. Very early in life, probably by a week old, it is necessary to see to the puppies' front claws, because by that time, especially if a large litter, they are causing the dam much discomfort by scratching at her breasts when feeding. If she is allowed to get sore breasts she may quite likely savage one of the pups, so avoid this trouble by shortening the extreme tips of every pup's claws with a pair of sharp scissors just as often as ever they begin to feel long. Be careful how you do it, and only snip the pointed tips off.

At three weeks the puppies should be getting the idea of how to lap food from a flat dish. They may first learn the way by licking the empty dish in which their dam has had one of her milky feeds. As soon as they show interest in this way, try them with a little warm milk and glucose, in a flat saucer till they learn to lap, which is usually in about two lessons. From them onwards, for their very first artificial feeds give them dried full cream milk powder diluted with hot water and a few spoonfuls of glucose. It should be mixed to the consistency of good cream. Any baby milkfood will do, such as Whelpi or Ostermilk, but for large litters it is best to order the full cream milk of some firm advertising in the dog papers. This will not be so expensive, and the milk powder is just as good; later on it can be diluted with cows milk. With a large litter it is particularly desirable to teach the puppies to lap as early as three weeks, for though they take but the smallest imaginable amount at a time it is a gradual help to the dam by supplementing her own milk supply to some extent. For by this age a large litter makes a heavy demand upon her. Feed each puppy separately with the diluted milk just warm but not hot, and give each only as much as it will lick off the saucer readily. At three and a half weeks this little routine should be undertaken twice a day, and is best done just before the dam returns from one of her airings, for two reasons; one being they are not then so ravenously hungry and waiting to tear at her, and the other that she will promptly clean up all their milky faces and any spillage there may have been.

When the pups are between three and four weeks old, many bitches have a habit of vomiting their own food for the family. It is a perfectly natural instinct for supplying the youngsters with pre-digested food till they are of an age to masticate their own, and those that do it are usually the best mothers. Even so it is not in the best interests of either mother or pups, and is best avoided by feeding her away out of sound of the pups and keeping her away from them for quite an hour after each of her meals. As even then a bitch may trick you and still manage to vomit a portion of her food, be very sure that every particle of her own diet at this stage has been minced very small. Tiny pups have been known to choke on lumps of meat or biscuit thrown up for them by an over-solicitous mother. After all it is not her fault – she means well!

Before they are three weeks old the pups should be on their feet, and their milk teeth will be coming through. If you have fed the mother well and supplemented the puppies' food as indicated, they should by this time be a lusty clamouring bunch, and the dam may be a trifle weary of their perpetual desire to feed from her. So do provide her with an adjacent bed for herself into which the pups cannot crawl, or a raised bench in front of the box, so that she can take refuge from them and rest unmolested if she wishes.

At the outset of founding a kennel, never be persuaded into buying a male dog, and do not be tempted to retain any of the dog puppies you may breed at first. If you get all dog and no bitch puppies in a litter, it is much wiser to sell the lot before they reach maturity and hope for some bitch pups next time. Should there be an outstanding dog pup among them he will doubtless find his own level in other and more experienced hands, and if he proves a show success the credit for having bred him is still yours. Retain the best bitch puppy generation after generation, and some day maybe the sensational dog pup will turn up. The dog which can go the top at championship shows, and thus demand considerable patronage at stud, is a rare product, and is usually the result of long continued striving after an ideal and many years of careful selection. Before your kennel is established it is a wasteful policy to keep a male dog, either home-bred or otherwise. It is far too easy to persuade oneself that he is worth using as a sire, thereby saving you stud fees; but it must be remembered that his opportunities in this direction will be very limited, his cost of keep all the year round for possibly only one or two litters by him is needless extravagance, and his blood-lines are unlikely to suit all your bitches alike. Moreover, unless you show him consistently and fearlessly up and down the country and gain the highest honours with him, no one else will want to use him so he cannot be said to be pulling his weight as an inmate of the kennel. Most of the best dogs in the breed are available at public stud, and the choice of a sire to suit your bitches is usually a wide one.

8

Puppy-Rearing

It has been said there is a champion in every litter if it were reared properly. This is exaggeration but much truth underlies it. Not everyone can rear Scot puppies successfully so that from their time of birth right on till they are ready to be trained to lead they have suffered no setbacks whatever. With forethought, common sense and unceasing attention to detail it is not difficult, provided the temperature of their place of birth has been adequate and artificial warmth whenever needed has been maintained on till they are two or three months old, longer in wintry weather. Warmth is every bit as essential for young puppies as food; in between mealtimes and short bouts of play they put in a terrific lot of sleep, and no puppy can sleep contentedly and profitably if it is cold.

At the age of three and a half weeks, maybe sooner, pups get the idea of lapping milk from a flat dish or saucer. As soon as they have learnt, the first feeds should be diluted milk, as described on page 125. Cow's milk alone, neither reduced nor with anything added to it, is quite unsuitable for young puppies. It is 87 per cent water, whereas the bitch's milk is only 75 per cent water, and is much richer in fats and other solids.

As soon as all the pups in a litter can lap readily, they must be offered little meals four times a day, to supplement the nourishment they are still getting from their dam; 8 a.m., 12 noon, 4 p.m. and 8 p.m. are the best times, and strict regularity is important. By degrees, add a little honey to the diluted milk, and to vary their diet suitably make alternations between the following items: Benger's food, Robinson's patent groats, raw egg beaten up in a little warm milk and sweetened with either sugar or honey, a plain baked milk pudding, an egg custard, or warm milk thickened with Farex or other similar preparation

(Thomas Fall)

Ch. Reanda Roger Rough

(Sally Anne Thompson)

Ch. Gaywyn Kingson

Kennelgarth family group

Left ro right: Venus, Ch. Mallich, Belita, Tweedledee, Croesus

Ch. Bidfield Bix

Ch. Glenview Sir Galahad

Int. Ch. Wyrebury Wrangler

(Sally Anne Thompson)

Ch. Gaywyn Likely Lad

Ch. Viewpark Pilot

made for babies. At one meal per day also add the necessary calcium powder. It is best to keep to milky feeds entirely until they are five weeks old.

At five weeks of age, accustom them gradually to the taste of good broth, which can be poured over wholemeal breadcrumbs or shredded wheat or wheatflakes, or thickened with Farex. By this time it is most important to feed each puppy separately. Only in this way can one be sure each is getting the same amount. It is extra trouble and entails cleaning several dishes instead of one, but those disinclined to take trouble should not be raising puppies. Each puppy's condition is the best guide as to whether it is getting the right amount. It should never be given enough to appear blown out after a meal, and whatever is offered it should be cleaned up utterly and eagerly. Never leave any food or dishes lying about.

At four-and-a-half to five weeks of age comes the big moment when the pups are introduced to good lean meat, preferably beef. This must at first be given in the form of scraped lean, raw. Cut a thin slice of raw lean, then lay it flat on a board and with the edge of a knife scrape away the pulp from the fibre. At first offer each pup a tiny helping of this pulp – not more than half a tea-spoonful – on your fingers. Later each can take it from a dish, separately and in turn. This should by now form one of the four meals in the day. At the end of the fifth week, the amount of scraped raw meat per puppy should be one teaspoonful. All amounts of food must be carefully regulated, for too much at any one meal can cause diarrhoea or indigestion.

By six weeks of age, the raw meat may be put through a fine mincer, or cut up into very very tiny pieces, instead of the scraped form. By this time two of their meals each day can be meat, one raw and one cooked. Always good lean meat, devoid of fat or gristle. If pups have been gradually accustomed to solid food in this way it will be found by six weeks they have but little more use for their dam except to sleep with at night. But that is a point to watch; some bitches become impatient with their pups by this age if left in a closed place with them all night, and at the first sign of her temper being tried too much she should only be with them for a spell last thing at night long enough for them to draw off her superfluous milk, and then returned to them first thing next morning for the same purpose. Many a pup has suffered

E

serious damage, and sometimes been killed by a dam who is allowed to become too bored with the insistent demands of a big litter.

So many people ask for a suggested diet sheet for puppies between the ages of six weeks and ten weeks that it may be helpful to set out the desirable foods in tabulated form, thus (alternate the various suggestions each day):

8 a.m.   Warm milk with glucose or sugar and Farex, Milk and egg, or scrambled eggs, or porridge with milk, etc.

12 noon.   Finely minced beef, mixed with soaked brown bread, rusks or puppy biscuits, sprinkled over with special feeding bonemeal.

4 p.m.   Repeat one of the 8 a.m. foods; but as the puppies grow older, give only a drink of sweetened milk.

9 p.m.   Minced cooked meat, chicken, rabbit or fish mixed with a small amount of soaked biscuit meal.

Late night: leave a drink of sweetened milk with Farex overnight, only if the dam is not with the puppies.

From about five weeks old onwards, pups will pick up and chew almost everything they come across, so the greatest watchfulness and forethought is needed to see that nothing lies about which can be harmful to them. They show a marked liking for coal and cinders, but must be prevented from getting any, for a sharp splinter of coal has been known to cause peritonitis. Anything they swallow – and they have no discretion at this age – other than the correct foods provided, can cause trouble, but since it is natural for them to try their teeth out on everything, it is wise to provide the safely trimmed sawn section of shin-bone, as described under the heading of Feeding in Chapter 6. Let the puppies have one or two of these only while the dam is away from them, and remove the bones before she returns. Puppies often chew the edges of their box, again running risk of swallowing damaging splinters of wood. In this case smear the chewed portions with an old creosote brush which has no creosote left on it but merely leaves a discouraging flavour behind. Toys of some sort should be provided for the same reason; things they can look upon as their own, carry into bed with them, or play with when so disposed. The selection of such things calls for forethought. If they are not given any it is small wonder they resort to tearing up whatever bedding is provided. They derive much amusement from a length of stout knotted rope, but some breeders argue that the tug-of-war resulting is bad for their mouths as it tends to make them undershot, and since rope can be chewed up and swallowed the best sort of plaything apart from the big beef bone is the indestructible variety of rubber toy made in the shape of a bone. As remarked earlier, balls are too dangerous, but the rubber bone not less than five inches long is too large to cause choking, gives the pups great delight carrying it around, and should last at least through the puppyhood of one litter, probably longer. As soon as any rubber toy shows the slightest sign of splitting or disintegrating, get rid of it at once.

In the pen or stall in which puppies are housed, the best way to encourage cleanly habits at the start is to spread newspaper down, always in the same corner, a corner furthest away from their bed. Once any of them have made use of the paper for sanitary purposes, the rest will soon follow suit, and before they are quite orderly in this respect it pays to leave a small portion of the soiled or wet paper down under the fresh piece provided. This only need be done a few times; it acts like a magnet in attracting them to the same spot to relieve themselves, and in consequence simplifies the frequent cleaning-up. Do not start using sawdust for them until quite nine months old.

Puppies from six weeks to six months of age require plenty of variety of diet. The only monotonous thing about it should be the regularity of their mealtimes. They should be fed four times a day until four months old, and from then on three times a day. If the pups are still in one's possession, it is wise to continue this till even nine months of age, for they are still growing and making substance. See that two consecutive meals are never the same and make sure that at least one meal per days consists of one of the three essentials, which are lean meat, raw eggs and fresh milk, remembering that if it is cow's milk it needs reducing or thickening before use. In addition to the four mealtimes, a late last drink of warm milk enriched with honey at about 11 p.m. or midnight is always a desirable nightcap for the youngsters. For the various supplementary foods, variety and nourishment can be provided by well-boiled rabbit, well-boiled tripe or sheeps' paunches, wholemeal bread rusks, shredded wheat soaked in gravy, groats or porridge oats, and plain milk puddings made with barley flakes or rice. As the pups grow, the liquid foods must become gradually less and the meat feeds given as dry as possible. One meal a day should still be of the milk variety, anyway until they are past six months old.

From a few weeks of age onwards, feeding-time offers the best possible opportunity for early training in respect of teaching each puppy its own name. Using a table or bench on which to feed each one separately, call one by name and then pick it up with two hands grasping the scruff of its neck and its tail and keep a gentle hold of the tail to steady the puppy while feeding on the table. As soon as that one has finished, lift it down to the floor again in the same manner and call the next one by name. They very quickly get to know their own identity in this way, while the extra handling involved gives them confidence in their handler, and in the hope that they may become show dogs ultimately it is essential to accustom them to this method of lifting. Never on any account lift a puppy by its forelegs or with hands grasping under its elbows. More fronts and shoulders are ruined in this way than one might suppose. In reverse, never drop a puppy on to either hind or forelegs first; place it down steadily with all four feet on the floor at once.

Practically every puppy that was ever born has round worms to some extent. If a puppy shows very early symptoms of being badly infested, such as by a pot-belly, discharge from the eyes, passing worms in its motions, or vomiting worms, it may have to be treated before the normal age. But whether or not any signs of worms are present, it should be a routine job to dose all puppies for worms between their sixth and seventh week. Failure to put on weight in later life can also be a sign of worms and tablets should be obtained from your veterinary surgeon who will supply these on the basis of the weight of the dog, so be sure to weigh your dog before asking him for worming tablets.

In more recent years a litter of puppies may have an odd 'swimmer' or splayed puppy. This is a condition where the puppy has great difficulty getting up on his back legs. Sometimes it's the front ones. No one seems to have the answer to why this should happen. Usually the puppy will right itself just by taking longer than his brothers and sisters to get on his feet. A little gentle exercise of the legs will help; only if the puppy shows no sign of improvement at 8–10 weeks should you contact your veterinary surgeon when usually a calcium injection will help. Never under any circumstances give up and allow the puppy to be put down.

Naturally there is more to the successful raising of puppies than just feeding and worming. Growing puppies need fresh air, sunshine, and a lot of sleep every bit as much as they need good food. The best time for them to play and romp is before each meal, and after meals they should be allowed to sleep undisturbed for quite an hour. Sunshine is the greatest tonic for them, with chance to seek shade if the weather is really hot; but never let direct sunlight fall on tiny pups under three weeks old; it is harmful to their eyes.

From two months to six months of age, every day should provide the growing youngsters with opportunity to run around and play in some spacious enclosure away from their own living quarters. Preferably twice a day. They need to stretch their legs and expand their lungs, and will eat and sleep all the better for doing so. If one or two adults in the kennel are known to be good-tempered and trustworthy, it is educational for puppies to mingle a little if possible with some of their elders. But such mixed parties must be supervised. If puppies are placed in an outdoor run on their own, a covered shelter must be provided into which they retire when sleepy or tired of playing, and they must never be left in such run long enough to become bored and to sit about doing nothing. In their waking hours both their minds and bodies need occupation. Too much confinement in one spot spells a dull mentality and may even cause shyness. If weather prevents any open-air freedom some days, it is well to carry indoors one puppy at a time for a short spell of human companionship, development of its own individuality and the experience of new sights and sounds. Pups which have had occasional access to the household kitchen, heard the clatter of washing-up, enjoyed the lick of a used plate, and discovered that human feet are things that may likely tread on one's toes unless one watches out, are more intelligently fitted for life than those without such experience. A puppy in the kitchen while any cooking is in progress, however, is *not* to be recommended, for boiling hot comestibles have been known to be spilt accidentally on a pup's back causing disastrous results.

By four months old each puppy should receive its first gentle experience of a collar and lead. This is quite a suitable wet-weather occupation, for the first feel of something around its neck can well be introduced as part of the general sense of fun and pleasure at being brought into the house. Above all, these early attempts at leading must be made happy and amusing for the pup, gradually encouraging it to view the whole proceeding as a special privilege. Never try to teach one pup to lead with the others around; they are all too ready to interfere, distract the pupil from concentrating on the business in hand, and in their own way to laugh at him for being all dressed up and looking funny, none of which helps his progress.

To omit to train every puppy to lead by four and a half to five months at the latest is really a form of indirect cruelty, for the promising youngster which may change hands at eight or nine months without ever knowing the feel of a collar and lead is probably in for a wretched time and much misunderstanding, and may never shape into the happy responsive show proposition its external virtues might indicate.

Equally necessary at this early age is the handling of each puppy. The earlier the weekly grooming, after about three weeks of age, becomes a routine, the better for their mental and physical well-being. Between three and four months their permanent teeth will be coming through, and a daily examination of mouths should ensure that all is proceeding normally. By four months of age the puppies should be given occasionally some dry crisp rusks, under supervision to be sure they neither quarrel nor choke, and the regular supply of big beef-bones is very essential at this stage. Both materially assist the process of teething, and if these have been supplied the pup's milk teeth will usually be pushed out and replaced by each new tooth without trouble. Sometimes, however, examination may prove that a milk tooth has remained too long in position causing the permanent tooth to be out of correct alignment. When this happens the offending milk tooth should be drawn without delay, otherwise the mouth may ultimately be faulty. The process of teething affects very much the temporary ear-carriage of Scot puppies. Even the precocious ones with ears stiffly erect from the earliest possible moment may drop them or carry them in all sorts of odd positions while teething, but they will usually recover the proper carriage when teething is finished at about six and a half months. Anxiety regarding ears becoming erect is not so prevalent nowadays as it used to be, but should an ear not be well up between seven and eight months it is time to do something to assist it. One of the best methods is to coat the whole surface of both front and back of the ear with collodion, holding the ear steadily in its correct position the while and until the application is quite dry and set. This causes no discomfort to the dog and usually one application or at most two will do the trick. The natural growth of the hair on the ears removes the dried collodion in due course.

The ultimate colour of eyes in our breed cannot be finally assessed till about four months of age. Mention of ultimate colouring must include a warning that wheaten coloured Scots have pink noses and pink pads to the feet at birth, and are often dark coated at first. These extremities darken and the coat colour lightens within a few days.

When some of the puppies are retained over the age of five months it is wise to house the sexes separately from then on. Bitches occasionally come on heat before six months old, and even if a litter brother does not manage a mating he will fret and lose interest in his food if one of his kennel-mates is on heat, and a young dog losing weight in this way is often very difficult to get back into good condition.

From six months onwards the youngsters should be gradually accustomed to adult routine, but their walks on the roads should be quite brief at first, only lengthening by gentle degrees, and it is best to continue giving them a light midday feed until quite nine months old in addition to their morning and evening meal, for they have much bulk and substance to build up and maintain.

Scottish Terriers need to be nicely rounded in their contours and well covered with flesh at every stage of their lives from the cradle to the grave. A puppy's condition reflects precisely the manner in which it has been reared. If it has received adequate bone-forming and body-building foods in judicious quantities and at regular hours, been kept warm enough when in, busy enough when out, and at all times clean and happy, it should never have a day off colour and should be a credit to its breeder. Few sights are more pitiable than an undernourished, thin and hungry puppy. Putting bulk and weight on the puppies does not necessitate overfeeding. On the contrary, too much food at any one meal can cause all sorts of ills. It is a matter of giving the right sort of foods in the right quantities and at the right times.

One often hears it said as an excuse for stringy-looking and even rickety puppies 'They are going through the thin lanky stage.' In our breed there is no necessity whatever for there to be such a stage. Admittedly it often comes about through diarrhoea resulting from a chill or from wrong feeding or from overfeeding, and it is a state far more easily acquired than cured. But it should be viewed as a sign of mismanagement somewhere, and need never happen. Really well-reared puppies from a healthy dam never have a day off colour, and make a gradual transition from the puppy fat of infancy to the muscular substance of adulthood without a check.

Puppy-rearing is not a pastime. That the pups themselves take it as a joke is all in their favour, but for the owner it should be a serious undertaking and a responsibility. Just as in breeding, and in planning the matings, he must be forever looking ahead, forestalling disasters, anticipating developments, alive to every possible contingency. A task of absorbing interest, exacting though it be.

9

The Stud Dog

As already pointed out, it is not an economical proposition for the small breeder or the beginner to keep a male dog. The temptation to do so is very great, especially as the dog puppies from a litter so often evince endearing qualities of temperament not always displayed by their sisters until a later age. But there comes a time in the affairs of dog-breeding when it is desirable to keep a stud dog, when the greatest care and thought should be given to his selection. It is well to remember that a far higher standard of perfection should be demanded of a dog used for breeding than of a bitch, since he may, given the opportunities, be responsible for upwards of a hundred puppies in a year as compared to the bitch's couple of litters at the most.

Convenience and the earning of stud fees are often put forward as reasons for keeping a dog for breeding, but no breeder will get very far in the exhibition world who is content to breed only 'convenient' puppies, while a dog needs to command considerable outside patronage at stud before his earnings justify his cost of keep.

Reasons for keeping a dog must be more sound than that; it may be that he supplies certain blood-lines necessary to a breeding scheme which cannot be obtained through a better dog elsewhere; or it may be that he is a worthy representative of illustrious parentage and for some reason is irreplaceable. In any case, the ideal stud dog should possess many important qualifications. He must be the son of a dam of some note and much merit; his pedigree should represent worthwhile influences and no weak links for at least seven or eight generations; and most essential of all he should possess the right, sane, confident, temperament. Preferably he should also be good in himself, able to prove his individual merits as a winner at championship shows, and last but by no means least he has to be a capable and virile stud dog, not only a proved stock-getter but with the ability to transmit his own dominant characteristics or those of his antecedents to his progeny. He must look essentially masculine. Most great sires possess a dominating personality and an air of assertiveness.

This may sound like a tall order, and naturally one meets with the occasional exceptions. Unsound and inferior dogs, quite useless for show, have in a few cases proved impressive sires, because they have the unseen gift of transmitting virtues inherent in their blood, but this is no justification for deliberately choosing such a dog for breeding. On the other hand there are examples in plenty of sensational winners and champion dogs which prove disappointing as sires, despite the innumerable opportunities coming their way. The acid test of a dog's capabilities at stud is the average quality of his stock from a variety of bitches.

A dog used at stud must be kept in absolutely tip-top condition, hard and muscular, neither too fat nor thin. He must have generous meat feeding, plus occasional raw eggs, and his exercise must be regular and adequate, as also must be his daily overhaul and grooming.

It is a mistake to mate a young dog until he is nine months old, and for his first bitch it is most important to use an experienced brood matron, one which is known to be amenable and easy to mate. A first experience with a bitch of this sort gives a young dog confidence in himself, and thereafter with bitches that are not so easy he will know what is expected of him. It is a wise rule not to let his second mating occur until he is twelve months old, and until he has reached nearly two years of age his bitches should not average more than one per month. This restriction pays in the long run, for Scottish Terriers are not fully matured till two years old, and a dog's virility and stock-getting ability will last all the longer if not overtaxed when young. During a busy period, a matured dog can serve perhaps two bitches per week for six weeks on end, but if worked as hard as this it is essential to give him a month's rest from stud work when the rush is over.

Train all young stud dogs right from the start to know that the bitch will be held for him to serve. When introduced to the bitch, it must first be discovered if she is pleased to meet him and inclined to encourage a little playful flirtation. If so, this is all in favour of effecting a happy mating, but should not be carried on long enough to waste a dog's energies and get him hot and panting. The moment the bitch shows willingness to stand for him, she should be firmly held by her collar with one hand, while the other hand supports her rear end unobtrusively and by slightly raising her vulva make it easier for the dog to penetrate. If the dog seems to have great difficulty in effecting penetration, the bitch must be examined for stricture. Smear some vaseline or similar grease on one finger of which the nail is filed down short and smooth and insert it into the bitch's vagina. A slight stricture is easily broken down in this way without using much force, but if there is an obstruction further up the passage it is a job for a veterinary surgeon before such a bitch can be mated.

When a bitch on examination appears to be in the right condition for mating and yet snaps viciously at the dog, no preliminary courtship should be allowed, and no chance of a second snap either, lest she damage the dog. Quite often a bitch behaving in this way at first, as most maiden bitches do, will react differently towards the dog the following day, if she has not passed the thirteenth day of her heat, so it is well to be patient and remove the dog till either some hours later the same day, or till the following day, and try again. Innumerable cases occur where on the second introduction to the dog a young bitch views the whole business from a different angle and positively welcomes the sight of the dog. Forced matings are seldom successful.

It is often imagined that a bitch will not conceive unless a tie has taken place. This is quite an erroneous belief, but the average stud dog owner prefers each mating to result in a tie, as being more satisfactory to all concerned. By a tie is meant the dog and bitch becoming firmly united, during which the dog turns round so that the two are back to back, and the bitch meantime must be restrained from sitting down, rolling over, or jerking and fidgeting unnecessarily. Whether a willing, or an unwilling bitch, she must be held all the time. Most breeders of Scots supervise the matings on a table or bench of a convenient height. And since the tie, if effected, may last anything from ten to fifty minutes, the resultant saving of backache for the owner is obvious, and preferable to adopting a prayerful pose on the floor for that length of time. The table or bench should be fairly spacious and preferably against a wall on two sides to avoid risk of the dog slipping over the edge. It is wise to supply a fibre mat to give a firm base for the dog's hind feet, and according to the varying heights of the bitches he may be required to mate, a set of short boards should be ready to hand, one or two of which can be slipped under the mat as requisite to raise him to the best level for his job.

When using the table method it is advisable for two persons to be present, because of the need to lift each animal from the table carefully when they separate. The bitch should be left in a quiet kennel to rest for an hour or so, with fresh drinking-water available; the dog should be returned to his own dwelling, given a raw egg beaten up in a drop of milk, and allowed to rest for two hours, likewise with a full waterbowl.

It is perhaps desirable to remind owners of stud dogs that before a mating the dog should have ample opportunity to relieve both bowels and bladder, and he should not be used until three hours have elapsed since his last meal. Very special care and consideration should at all times be given to a valuable stud dog. During his matings it is his comfort and convenience that must be studied before that of the bitch. He may have a reputation to maintain, and unless all his sexual undertakings are made as pleasurable as possible his enthusiasm may cool off.

Two services are not desirable if the first one has been successful, but where the first tie has been very brief or it has been agreed beforehand to give a bitch two matings, the second should occur under twenty-four hours. Stud fees should be paid in advance or at the time of mating, and are in all cases payable for the services of the dog irrespective of whether puppies result or not. Most owners of stud dogs willingly give a free service at her next heat should the bitch miss, but this is by no means compulsory and should be mentioned and agreed upon at the time of the first service. Sometimes the owner of a stud dog may agree to take a puppy from the litter in lieu of stud fee, and when this is arranged the whole agreement should be in writing, especially the exact age at which the puppy is to be taken over, sex of puppy and whether first or second pick of the litter. This arrangement is not really a profitable one for the owner of a bitch, for the value of a well-reared puppy of either sex in these days is twice if not three times as much as the average stud fee; moreover the sale of some of the litter may be missed or delayed by the failure of the dog's owner to make his choice or collect his puppy at the appointed time.

If issuing a printed stud-card for a dog or dogs, be sure to make it an accurate and comprehensive presentation of all the facts a fellow-breeder is likely to want to know. It should include the pedigree for not less than four generations, the dog's K.C.S.B. number if he has one, his Male Line symbol and his Family number, also his K.C. Registration number. Other essential facts are the name of the nearest railway station along with address and telephone number, while if space allows add the names of any winning progeny sired, besides a few Press reports on the dog himself written by well-known judges. If a photograph is included, for pity's sake let it be an individual and characteristic portrait, natural and alive-looking, rather than one of the touched-up wooden-dummy sort of reproductions which are made to appear all so much alike they are practically interchangeable. This latter kind cut no ice with the searcher after truth, who is well aware the dog in question could not by any stretch of the imagination resemble the picture, since in many cases it is anatomically impossible for any living animal to do so.

10

Preparation for Show

ONE of the ultimate aims of a breeder is the success of his stock in the show-ring, since it is the only available criterion of merit. It is also the aim of a number of other people who do not claim to be breeders but who have a flair for spotting a good young terrier and the ability to present it in a show to the best advantage.

It is not enough that a terrier should be a fairly near approach to the Standard and be in robust health, to make exhibiting it worth while. Taking these details for granted, there are many other factors which have nearly if not quite as much bearing upon success or failure at a show. Assuming a puppy has been brought up on the lines suggested in the section on Training in Chapter 6, so that it is responsive, alert and happy when on a lead, the early foundations towards show preparation will have been well and truly laid. Wisest are the breeders who endeavour to turn out this type of puppy, for buyers may then confidently expect from them terriers possessing what is called the show temperament and the rudiments of a sound education.

Naturally temperaments vary somewhat with each individual, and while the show training of one dog may take two or three months or longer before perfection of demeanour is attained, others may prove such apt pupils that they absorb all the necessary knowledge in as many weeks. One can seldom, however, prepare a dog's coat to be fit for show in a matter of a few weeks, so the coat preparation and the training of the dog's mind should proceed hand in hand. Training a responsive terrier for good ring deportment is one of the most fascinating of occupations. This, together with the daily attention to the dog's coat, makes the whole process of show preparation one of the most interesting of the many tasks performed by a dog owner. It requires concentration, perseverance and confidence.

Concentration, particularly upon the dog itself during every lesson given. It is no use taking the dog around to give it experience and then becoming engrossed in conversation with a friend and ignoring the dog's reactions meanwhile to new sights and sounds. If it is an outing primarily for the dog's education, the dog is the only being of importance at the time, and his demeanour must be considered from start to finish. Concentration on his condition and his coat is also needed day in, day out, because on his ultimate presentation in the show-ring he must be looking his very best.

Perseverance, plus patience will ensure that the schooling and the trimmings are maintained day after day in spite of the setbacks that may occur.

Confidence, is perhaps the quality most needed in one who sets out to train and show a dog, for the trainer must have enough for himself and the dog too. The dog looks to the trainer, needs to feel that he is a person who can at all times be trusted, and who can reassure one if one happens to be a little dog in momentary doubt.

With a puppy, say between six and eight months, a short lesson in ring demeanour must be given every day – more often if time allows. At first, each lesson should only be of five minutes' duration. The first approach to the dog in its kennel should be made with a lightweight narrow show collar and long lead in hand, and some small bits of boiled or baked and dried liver in the right-hand pocket. Attach the lead to the dog, with words of encouragement and a bit of liver as bait, and take it to some place away from other dogs where there is enough space to walk up and down from end to end as well as round in a circle. With the lead in the left hand, encourage the dog to move at the normal walking pace of a human being, keeping always on your left side and not pulling either forwards, backwards or sideways. At the first suitable response, moving nicely, reward it with a bit of liver. Any tendency to pull must be discouraged by a sharp jerk on the lead and no reward. The aim is to have the dog trotting gaily alongside on a fairly slack lead, the lead not so slack that it gets mixed up with the dog's feet but slack enough to allow the place of its attachment to the collar to drop to the side of or under the dog's face. Nothing looks worse than a Scot being nearly strangled by a tight lead held vertically above its head; when seen thus in a show-ring it invariably means one of two things – either the dog has never been trained to lead properly or its handler is trying to hide faults in its front action.

Accustom the dog to moving round in a circle to the left, as if the place was a show-ring, the dog on the inner side and led by the left hand. Upon the successful and smooth performance of each circle reward him. Then practise moving him in a straight line from end to end of the room, lawn, or enclosure, and by means of light control on the fairly slack lead teach him to turn at the end and move straight back again in the opposite direction. Give reward every time when it is deserved and never when it is not. Then, as you come to a halt, teach the dog with a softly spoken word of command to stand still, ears and tail up, watching for the reward which will, if earned, be supplied from your pocket. Never reward until he is standing properly and looking alert, but never miss doing so promptly every time he adopts this correct attitude. Take another couple of turns round the imaginary ring, then stop again to practice the standing to attention. The tendency often is, when expected to stand still, the dog will sit or drop its tail, but if enough concentration has been given to bestowing due reward at only the right moments it can be trained to stand and enjoy standing. If any pupil, in spite of training, still shows an inclination to sit when he should be standing, just step a pace or two towards him as if you were going to walk on to him, and this will quickly put him on his feet again. Some youngsters, when being trained to stand, have a habit of springing into the air, or rearing like a horse, in which case drop the loose lead a little further to allow of your slipping one foot over the lead on the floor, within a foot of the dog's neck, so that when he next tries a wild jump he will come a cropper on to his chin, so is unlikely to attempt it many more times.

All lessons at first should be very brief, never continuing long enough for either the dog's or the trainer's interest to flag, for if it does more is lost than gained. At each short practise one should be able to see an improvement. On every occasion the whole experience must be a happy one for the dog, so that in his mind the joy of being singled out, put on a lead and rewarded each time he tries to play its part, are forever closely associated incidents. He will soon learn to take a pride in showing himself off. At the conclusion of each short lesson he should be put back in his kennel at the same time as taking off his collar and lead.

When these short lessons have been repeated often enough for the required behaviour of the pupil to have become practically second nature, introduce a table into the imaginary ring, and if possible get other people to handle the dog on the table, giving him bits of liver while they do so. It is also useful preparation for the show experience later on.

This preliminary training at home should serve to establish the dog's complete confidence in its handler, and the next step must be to gradually apply tests of his behaviour in the form of outside influences. He may first be taken to a moderately quiet road where an occasional car or passer-by may or may not distract his attention. After that, he has got to be accustomed to every kind of sight and sound possible so should be taken around somewhere every day till such things as road traffic, groups of people, railways stations, busy shops and so forth find him quite unperturbed. The more new experiences of life he gets the better. These should include some car travel, for it is likely his first journey to a show will be in a car. It should also entail being boxed for short intervals now and again, for if he travels by rail to a show he must accept being boxed as part of the normal routine. All these preliminaries are part of his necessary education as a self-possessed show terrier.

Country-dwellers have to work a little harder than town-dwellers to attain good results with their show candidate, for the latter can usually accustom a dog to new sights and sounds without going very far. In the country, however, no opportunity must be missed which can possibly be utilized as part of the training. A ride in a car or bus, a call at the village store, introduction to every stranger who comes to the house – all these can be made educational if the dog is rewarded and praised the while. One so often hears the moan, 'My dogs see so few people', or 'He shows beautifully at home', but these handicaps can so easily be overcome if the right methods are employed. It is essential as often as possible to put the pupil through his ring performance on strange ground and in surroundings that are new to him. With the usual supply of liver in the pocket, be sure you can get the dog's attention any time in spite of external distractions. Use, whenever possible, the presence of any and all people who come to the house, by fetching along and displaying the prospective show terrier on a lead. Don't let it worry you if they take no

F

interest and don't want to see the animal, it is good for the animal to take a look at them. By this means one impresses on the dog's mind that the company of strangers means show-ring ritual and a happy interlude on a lead. Many owners find the public bar at their local inn one of the best aids in schooling a youngster. Long years ago when I had a big kennel and not enough time to train all the young stock, a friend in a Scottish mining village used to take one for me occasionally to accustom it to life in general. As they always returned to me bubbling over with self-assurance I once asked him the recipe for this very sound build-up of character. The reply was, 'A pub crawl every night and a football match on Saturdays'! And one could do a lot worse, for every such experience is broadening to a dog's mind so that the noise and bustle of a show when he gets to one will find his calm quite unshaken. It militates sadly against one's chances of success, and is unfair both to the dog and to the judge on the day, to take an untutored dog into a ring, so it is well to spare no pains over its education.

One of the aids towards bright keen show demeanour on the part of a terrier is to kennel him in the indoor wall-pen or roomy sleeping-box for anyway the latter part of his show preparation. The effect is a psychological one. A dog being trained to show soon learns to associate the appearance of his handler plus lead and liver with his release from a moderately small compartment, and he is all the more eager. As time goes on, during his trimming which is part and parcel of show preparation, the wall-pen also has advantages; certain parts of the coat may need special treatment, and this is likely to be more effective when the subject is kennelled alone and under fairly close observation.

Far be it from me to advocate close or prolonged confinement for any dog. To overdo such a method of kennelling is to defeat its own object, for the mentality of the inmate subjected to it for too long periods will become dulled. 'All work and no play, etc.' But in the last stages of converting a half-educated dog into an aspirant to high show honours, a few weeks restriction of his kennel space and his freedom are usually all that is necessary. Needless to say, every dog undergoing this intensive schooling must be given his regular exercise. Part of this will be on the lead while he is seeing something of the outside world, and in addition he should never miss the daily leg-stretch and free lung-expanding gallop. During show preparation, however, this latter gambol must be under supervision, otherwise some of the labour and time expended on the coat in readiness for a show may be wasted. Indubitably our breed is first and foremost a working breed, but just as we could not expect an industrious land-girl to come straight from the fields to compete in a beauty competition without first getting all dolled up, so we cannot expect our terriers to display all their physical attributes to the best advantage in the somewhat unnatural environment of a show-ring if they have just been indulging in a rabbit hunt or a burrowing contest.

This recommendation towards a certain amount of judicious restraint is put forward mainly for the guidance of the novice exhibitor, for examples at shows are only too numerous of the beginner's dog which could have gone higher had it been better disciplined for a few weeks prior to the show. And by discipline in this case is meant a routine of being boxed or housed in a small pen for short periods some part of every day. Many novices seem to think if they have taught their exhibit to lead and have dealt with its trimming they can let it drift around loose all day at home and yet expect it to put up a creditable performance in a ring.

Long before a show daily attention must be given to the coat of the prospective exhibit. Dogs cast their dead coats every six months, and bitches at the time they have, or could have had, puppies. Most coats become ready for stripping for the first time between seven and eight months of age. Before the outer coat actually falls off it is quite dead and loose, so is much better removed evenly all over by finger and thumb, when the new jacket which is waiting to come through will grow all the better. There is, however, an art, in stripping our breed to attain the best effect.

The art lies in the removal of the dead outer coat from certain portions of the animal before other portions. Leaving an old coat on has the natural effect of retarding the growth of the new, consequently good use can be made of this fact to bring about the desired result in the finished article. Skilful stripping is thus a task not to be hurried but done in gradual stages.

Reference to the accompanying diagram (A) will indicate the sequence to be followed. Groom the dog very thoroughly before starting to strip him. Have a little powdered resin handy in which to dip the tips of first-finger and thumb. This give one a better grip on the hairs to be pulled. Then, with finger and thumb taking hold of a very few hairs at a time, strip the dead longer hairs only from the legs, underbody, and tail (Section 1 in diagram). Pull every hair the 'way of the wool' – that is in the direction in which it lies, never the reverse way. Do not be too drastic towards the root of the tail. A tail can always be shaped out nicely during the subsequent trimming.

It is as essential to remove the dead outer coat from underbody and legs periodically in this way as it is from other parts of the dog. Like the remainder, it is dead every six months, and if left on it merely retards the growth of new hair. Some fear to remove it thinking they are sacrificing good furnishings, but actually dead furnishings left on sacrifice themselves in the long run, for

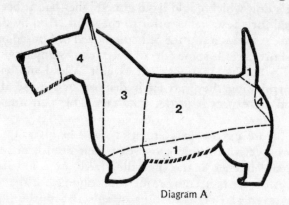

Diagram A

instead of becoming new growth of harsh hair, just at the time they are most wanted they will be found to be a tangled muddle of old and new hair mixed, difficult to trim satisfactorily. That is the whole object of starting early with these portions alluded to (Section 1) and allowing enough time for them to start new growth before going on to the next section.

Individuals vary slightly in their rate of coat growth, but as a general rule quite six weeks should elapse before starting to strip the ribs, loin, and back (Section 2). Proceed in the same way as before, gripping only a few hairs at a time. If the coat is definitely dead, as it should be before stripping, this area is a lot easier to deal with than the first, and in expert hands takes but a few minutes. Always when stripping, steady the skin of the dog with the free hand, so that the portion of skin from which hair is being pulled is always taut at the time. This not only aids the work but is vastly more comfortable for the dog. Do not be tempted to go beyond the area indicated by the dotted lines for Section 2. If the dog has to go around looking a bit of a freak for a few weeks, who should worry? – it is all in a good cause. Should the ignorant poke fun at him retaliate with the old proverb 'Let those laugh that win' and invite them after the show to take a look at the red prize cards.

Another three weeks must be allowed to pass before dealing with the back of the neck and the shoulders (Section 3 in diagram). By this time the leg and underbody hair should have started to make new growth and this can be greatly assisted by daily vigorous brushing with a stiff-bristled brush.

The last portions (Section 4 in the diagram A) can now be cleaned off, but not by finger-and-thumb stripping. As being more merciful to the dog, clippers are used on the ears, the skull portion of the head, the throat and front of neck and just under the tail. And the use of clippers brings us to the final part of show preparation, the trimming. But first some mention must be made of the fact that it is really not in the best interests of a good coat to strip it off at any time *other* than when it is dead. If for some reason it has to be done at another time, the use of a stripping knife will be necessary. There are innumerable makes on the market. One with a finely serrated edge is best. Use it by placing the thumb along the blade and grasping the hairs to be pulled between the knife and the thumb. In this case you work with the dog's head pointing away from you, not as in hand-stripping with his head towards you. Be sure to keep the skin of the dog taut the while, with your other hand. This kind of forcible stripping is usually done wholesale – all over the dog at one time – mainly for the one-dog owner who prefers his pet to look barbered, but quite often by the impatient exhibitors who will not allow time for the coat to ever reach its natural length. By doing this repeatedly, removing fast hairs by force that are not dead and ready to come off, the coat is deprived of its right to undergo the normal change from old to new which is a health-giving process. Naturally some tidying-up of a dog in full coat can be done to keep him presentable at any stage of his coat growth; by shortening a few overlong hairs at their tips with the stripping-knife, and by keeping the skull, throat, ears and tail neat with clippers and scissors. Indeed, the frequency of championship shows decrees that successful exhibits are often kept in good show form as regards coat for probably nine months out of the twelve. This can be done with good coats, those that are dense, really harsh in texture, and flat-lying. But a forced all-over stripping at the wrong time can ruin even a good coat, while the indifferent coats are none the better for it. The too-profuse coat, very prevalent in these days, is only at its best for show when, after stripping at the normal time, the new outer coat has reached the desired length and is still fast.

Where the outer coat has been removed by correctly timed stripping, the stripped portions should be clad in a close furry undercoat, so dense that the skin cannot be seen through it. It should be remembered that the undercoat needs to be shed and renewed just as the outercoat, but it is a mistake to comb away too much undercoat until the new outercoat is showing through. At that stage, superfluous undercoat will be dead and can be scraped off either with a wire-bristled brush, a fine comb or a tool resembling the curry-comb used on a horse. The dog forcibly stripped at the wrong time is bereft of all protective covering, for no undercoat will be apparent at first, and his ultimate state never results in the same healthy bloom shown by a coat stripped at the natural time. Our aim in stripping should be to assist Nature, not oppose it.

If stripping is an art, then indeed trimming for show is a fine art, requiring a deal of practise. One has to accept the fact that it is done with intent to decive. It is intended to enhance good features and disguise bad ones. Skilful trimming can make a head look longer, a neck appear more shapely, the shoulders cleaner, the front straighter, and the back and tail shorter then they actually are. It can thus be appreciated that the expert trimmer wields a very powerful weapon against competitive attack. He cannot by trimming alone make a bad dog look like a good done, but he can make a mediocre dog appear to be a whole heap better than it really is, which is so often the reason for some show awards seeming puzzling to the ringsider. Judges are not infallible, and it not infrequently happens in keen competition that the better specimen not so carefully prepared loses to a less sound terrier beautifully presented. Since some judges are thus swayed by show presentation it behoves the ambitious exhibitors to learn all they can about trimming.

The trimmer should work with a mind attuned to the Standard description of the ideal dog, for the Standard is the yardstick by which one's dogs have to be measured. If they do not by nature fit the description laid down, that is where artificiality in the form of trimming steps in.

The tools employed in trimming are many and various. Some good quality clippers are essential, also a pair of hairdresser's scissors kept very sharp, and a pair of thinning scissors. The average owner by the time stripping is mastered will no doubt have acquired all sorts of different types of stripping-knives, and one of these comes into use during trimming, as also does a coarse file for the nails. The successful use of clippers requires considerable practise, but some skill can be attained in time. The beginners should experiment on a dog which is not going to be shown

Diagram B

and if possible pick up some hints from a practical demonstration also.

When using clippers, always work against the growth of the hair, and point the clippers at a fairly sharp angle against the skin – not lying flat. Also, attempt only to utilize about one-third of their cutting surface; cut as it were with only a corner of the clippers at a time. A more even result is obtained this way.

The accompanying sketch (B) indicates by the light unshaded portions where the hair is kept quite short. This necessitates the use of clippers for the skull, the throat, part way down the front of the neck, and the backs of the ears if they are the hairy sort of ears. The edges of the ears and the tapering of the tail are done by trimming very carefully with scissors. Some use clippers for the seat portion below the tail, while others get as good an effect with scissors and a trimming-knife.

If a start is made at the head, imagine a line across the skull from ear to ear, and clip forward from that line towards the eyebrows, being careful not to go too close to the eyebrows. These are trimmed to shape later with the aid of the trimming-knife. Next, from just above the projecting breastbone clip upwards to throat. Imagine a line drawn round the dog's face just behind his eyes and passing round his muzzle, the upper section of this imaginary circle being very slightly to the rear of the lower section. Never clip beyond this line forwards. It is indicated in the sketch on p. 151 where the black shading represents the profuse hair left on the foreface.

Imagine another line drawn from the base of the ear downwards towards the front of the attachment of the foreleg. This line is also indicated in the sketch by contrasting light (clipped) and dark (unclipped) portions. A rough guide to the whereabouts of this imaginary line on the dog is supplied by the ruff or frill of hair he grows in a natural state, where the front neck hair and the body hair meet. Clip in an upward direction, against the coat growth, within these imaginary lines, but be very sure not to travel too far with the clippers. It is far better to err the other way, for once hair is cut off it cannot be put back. At the junction of face and neck, near the jawbone, it is usually found the hair tends to grow in varying directions, so when clipping here and on the cheeks one has to vary the angle of approach with the clippers so that the cutting takes place always *against* the lie of the coat.

The next task is to grade off nicely with a trimming-knife the places of junction between the clipped and the unclipped parts of the coat. The object is to effectually hide any obvious contrast between the two. The dense coat clothing the back of the neck has to be blended in to the short cut hair on sides and front of neck, and in the same way trim from the short hair down the front of the neck into the longer hair around the shoulders and on the brisket so that the short merges into the long in as natural seeming a manner as possible.

The whole art of successful trimming lies in bringing about this apparent merging of the shorter into the longer coat without showing any lines of demarcation between the two. If clipping the portion below the tail, the same blending of longer into shorter coat must be carried out with the trimming-knife so that the set-on of tail and nicely rounded quarters are shown to advantage. The tail itself can be partly dealt with by a trimming-knife near its root, but the root should be thick, and if not thick by nature a dense growth of hair for its first couple of inches gives the desired impression. Further up towards the tip it is easier and less painful for the dog to use scissors and taper it off to a fine point. In the same way as with clippers, when using scissors cut always into and against the lie of the hair, as the effect is more natural.

The edges of the ears must be trimmed round closely but very carefully with sharp scissors. It is all too easy to snip a bit of flesh when tackling the outer edges of the ears near the lobe, which causes profuse bleeding and a resentful dog, so be warned. Leave a little fullness of hair just in front of the base of the ears, as this makes them appear smaller. Trim the eyebrows very lightly with the trimming-knife so that they blend into the cut hair of the skull and are encouraged to lie forwards, not upwards. Every dog's head varies somewhat, so the eyebrow trimming must be governed by whatever shows his expression to the best advantage. In the same way with a trimming-knife, graduate the meeting-place of short and long hair under the muzzle. Some people go a lot too far forward with the clippers under the foreface, resulting in a grotesque beard being left only on the chin resembling a boat. This does not help the necessary depth of foreface. Others have a habit of cleaning out the hair far too closely between the eyes. Certainly it is usually necessary to remove a moderate amount here, as nothing looks worse than a fuzz of hair between the eyes, and though it may be only an optical illusion, a clear-cut stop enhances the apparent depth of foreface. But as in the whole art of trimming, it is better to do nothing to excess, but to try and make the finished product look as natural as possible, as if its coat had actually grown the way it appears on show day.

When shortening the hair on the area linking up the front of the neck with the shoulders, working downwards with a trim-ming-knife, carry on down a little further than the elbow joint on the outer side of the foreleg. Most Scots tend to grow a pro-fusion of hair in this region, which may give an impression when coming towards you that the dog is out at elbows. He may be, too, in which case this bit of trimming must be all the closer.

much can be done legitimately to improve the appearance of the front. In all cases the growth of hair on the legs should be kept as uniform as possible, consisting of hairs of the same average length, which ought to be moderately profuse, bushy and wiry, to give the impression of heavy bone whether it is present or not. Shorten the tips of any overlong spikes of hair on the legs, as these detract from the solid appearance. Minor failings on the part of either front or back legs can be skilfully disguised to some extent by trimming. As regards the forelegs the aim is to make them appear straight when viewed either from the front or the side, so it is usually desirable to shorten a little the hair on the inside of the foreleg at the pastern joint while leaving it compensatingly thick on the outer side of the leg at the same level. Trim the feathering which grows down the back of the foreleg so that it has an even appearance. At the hocks, shorten any too-long hairs, and if the dog moves too close behind clean away some hair from the inside of the hock joints and from the outer sides of the rear feet. Conversely, if the dog is too wide behind, the fault can be hidden somewhat by leaving more hair between the hocks and trimming fairly close down the outer sides of the hind legs.

Feet, both fore and aft, must all be neatly trimmed as to the hair, cutting back slightly with scissors any uneven growth so that each foot appears compact and rounded, and regular attention must be given to the nails of a show dog. Whether or not the dog is a good mover blessed with round well-padded feet which cause him to keep his own nails ship-shape by his road exercise, it is well to look to the nails of a prospective exhibit two or three times a week, and a brief rub with a carpenter's coarse file will prevent any one nail becoming longer than others. This attention will maintain the shape of a good foot while improving the less good.

The two silhouettes on p. 155, 'C' and 'D', are built up on the same framework and serve to illustrate the amount of alteration in general appearance which could be effected by trimming a poor-coated specimen. Unfortunately many present-day dogs when quite untrimmed could conceivably resemble 'C', yet their outline can by trimming be made to resemble 'D'. Readers can decide for themselves which of the two suggests the nearest approach to the standard.

In the best interests of the Scottish Terrier, breeders would do well to give as much, if not more, attention to selecting for the right coat texture as they do to other points. The harsh, double, close-fitting and flat-lying coat which on no part of the dog exceeds two inches in length in an absolutely natural state, is one of the best characteristics of our hardy, workmanlike breed, and is the feature which renders him the serviceable companion of man in every kind of weather. The popularity of a breed is inevitably endangered when a stage is reached in its evolution that too much dependence is placed upon artificiality and too little on

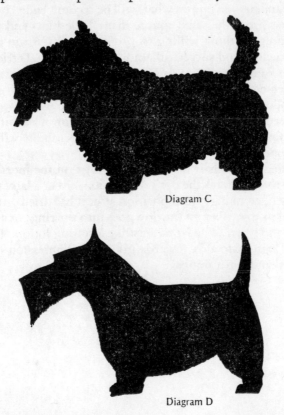

Diagram C

Diagram D

sheer merit. A good deal of the responsibility rests with the judges, who can penalize soft hair and excessive trimming as readily as they should reward the correct coat texture when they meet with it.

It has been truly said that no dog is well trimmed that shows signs of having been trimmed. When shown he should give the impression that his coat always looks exactly as it does then, the coat of a well-brushed and groomed working terrier, clad in hard hair from stem to stern. The better the coat the more surely can this ideal be attained.

One cannot expect to attain proficiency in trimming at first. It needs patience and takes time. At different stages in one's career as an exhibitor of dogs, every imaginable sort of knife, comb, trimming gadget, including safety-razors, wax-tapers for singeing and heaven knows what, will be recommended by fellow-exhibitors. From the same source many little hints and tips may be picked up by those willing to profit by them, for in the main the experienced and successful among the Scottish Terrier fraternity have a genuine desire to help the beginner. And it is always well to remember one is never too old to learn.

The following tips concerning coats may be useful.

To speed up growth of hair on any portion where it is most needed, few things are better than brisk brushing with a stiff brush dipped in rain water.

To stiffen up the hair on foreface or legs on the morning of a show, so that it retains the desired position, either a lather of soap can be used, combing it into position after it has dried on the hair, and needless to say before the dog goes into the ring; or a mixture of sugar and water. The latter acts like a setting lotion. These are perfectly legitimate aids towards giving an impression of better 'whiskers' and 'furnishings'.

Exhibiting

THERE are some owners who, for business or health reasons, cannot devote the time necessary for preparing and handling their own exhibits. There are others who, try as they may, never attain that degree of skill in presentation which is essential to successful dog showing. Some handle expertly but their trimming is too drastic and obvious; some trim to perfection but come to grief as handlers. Again, there is a small section of the dog-owning community who can negotiate all the tricky fences of show preparation and yet fail at the last ditch – the show-ring – purely through lack of self-confidence.

Such people need not necessarily be deprived of the satisfaction of seeing their exhibits winning high honours in the show-ring provided they have a dog good enough, for this is where the services of a professional handler can be employed. It is a costly proceeding, naturally, for no handler can be expected to do justice to a prospective exhibit unless he or she has it in their care for many weeks – maybe months – prior to a show, during which time all the processes of training and trimming will be carried out expertly and a weekly charge made for this and the dog's keep. On top of that there is a scale of charges for the actual handling at the shows. The owner, however, is spared the necessity and expense of attending the shows in question should he be too disinterested or too busy to do so.

There are conflicting opinions as to the desirability or otherwise of placing one's dog with a handler. Quite a number of our breed have become champions in professional hands which would never have done so otherwise. This is not to suggest the mediocrity of the specimens so handled but rather the ability of the average professional not only to present the terrier to advantage but to extract from it that last ounce of showing capacity which often tips the scale in its favour. As against that, the amateur owner in possession of a good dog who personally prepares and pilots it to the top unaided, till that gladsome day when the coveted title of 'Ch' can precede its name, experiences a joy and satisfaction which transcends all the other delights of dog-owning. The thrill of winning with a youngster one has bred, schooled and put down fit for show is something only the true dog lover can fully appreciate, and it is within the reach of all who have the health, the time, the inclination and the temperament. Dog showing is one of the few sports where the amateur and the professional start level and have an equal chance of success.

It is assumed the intending exhibitor will first have visited a few dog shows and got a general idea of what goes on at such events. The weekly canine papers can be consulted as to the whereabouts and dates of forthcoming shows, and until you are known as a regular exhibitor you have to apply to the Show Secretary concerned for a schedule. This acquired, make a note of the date for closing entries, and if the classification includes a class or two suitable for your exhihibit, fill in the entry form very clearly and accurately, enclose the fees required and be sure to post by the stated date.

At the outset it is best not to fly too high. Most districts can boast of a local canine society, and the small Members or Limited shows organized by such Clubs cater mainly for either dogs or owners or both, who are beginners. Read the class definitions carefully, and even if no class is scheduled for the breed, an initial venture into an Any Variety Terrier class, or an Any Variety Maiden, offers a chance to gain useful experience for both owner and exhibit. The drawback to these little shows is usually the absence of benching, so that the dog has no place to call his own while awaiting his classes. The practised owner takes a light-weight travelling-box into the show for the dog to occupy when not in the ring. If attending a benched show remember a stout collar and benching chain will be required for securing the dog on his bench.

Before a dog can be shown he has to be registered with a name of his own at the Kennel Club, and it should be observed that when signing an entry form one is undertaking to abide by all rules of the Kennel Club, which is the governing body of dogdom. If you have bought the dog and it is already registered, make sure his transfer of ownership is put through the Kennel Club before entering him for a show. Moreover, if the dog has done any previous winning it is important to get his list of wins in detail from the previous owner, otherwise you may enter him in classes for which he is ineligible and later have to forfeit your prize-money (if any).

Whatever type of show is selected, when it is the dog's first experience it is best to carry him through the show entrance and on to the veterinary surgeon's table, for the first requirement is for him to be 'vetted'. Many a promising puppy has received altogether the wrong first impressions of a show by either being trodden on going through the crowded entrance door or snapped at by another dog. It is so very important that all the early associations in the dog's mind relating to being shown are happy ones, for first impressions are apt to be lasting, so you cannot be too careful to guard against mishaps at the start of his career. After a few shows, most Scots look upon them as thoroughly enjoyable outings, if they have been wisely handled, and on being led through the crowds amidst all the noise adopt a nonchalant 'couldn't care less' attitude befitting a philosophical Diehard.

The larger shows usually issue an exhibitor's pass and re-moval order, with the number for your dog stated thereon, several days prior to the show. It is helpful to memorize the number. It will be needed as you pass the entrance, again for the veterinary examination, and definitely as you search for the appropriate bench; while it saves the ring-steward trouble when judging starts if you quote your dog's number to him as he hands out the ring-cards.

Overnight, it is well to assemble everything you will need to take with you on the day, so that you may start off in good time, calm, cool and collected. Of primary importance are: the dog itself on a collar and lead, a show-lead, a bench-chain, a dog-comb, a drinking-bowl, the admission pass, some boiled liver ready cut up and dried enough to go in your pocket, and enough loose cash handy with which to buy a catalogue. Have the pass, the cash, the comb and the liver in easily accessible pockets. Secondary considerations are: a blanket or rug for the dog's bench if it be cold weather, some form of dog-brush, a bottle of water or milk and water, a pin for fixing your ring-number, and a pencil. Often the drinking-water supply at a show is a long walk from the benches, hence the desirability of taking enough with you for the dog to quench his thirst anyway on arrival. A very useful addition to the outfit is a string net for spreading across the front of the bench. These can be obtained from any canine suppliers. While not in the least impeding the general public's view of your dog, it prevents his being stroked or handled by all and sundry, and since this is one way infection is spread at a show a net is a very worthwhile investment.

Be sure to reach the show at least half an hour before the scheduled time for arrival. If the dog journeys there in a box, do not feed him near the time of starting from home, but quite two hours earlier, if at all, and give him every chance to empty his bowels and bladder before you set off and again before entering the show hall or ground. At indoor shows this is more than ever important, for many a fine show venue has been lost to canine societies by the sheer carelessness of exhibitors allowing their dogs to foul the hall because they were too slack or in too much of a hurry to make sure these jobs had been done outside.

The evening before a show, always feed your exhibit very sparingly, so that he will be all the more keen about the boiled liver in the ring on show day.

The first thing to do on arrival is to bench your dog, attaching him comfortably and securely by means of the correct sort of benching-chain which has a swivel at both ends. Arrange this so that the dog has only enough reach to turn himself round, but never enough to permit of his head stretching as far as the front edge of the bench. Likewise adjust it low enough (to the ring provided for the purpose) so that the dog cannot jump upwards.

One has only to walk around any of the big shows to realize the stupidity and lack of imagination indicated by the manner in which a lot of the exhibits are chained, causing accidents which should have been avoided. Often it will be found that the bench partitions do not fit closely against the back boarding, but expose a wide crack through which a tail, or even a nose, can be pushed. The dog on the next bench has every right to resent it if a portion of his neighbour's anatomy appears through this crack, so use fore-thought and take the precaution of stuffing up this crack with whatever comes to hand – the dog's blanket or your overcoat perhaps; even the sacrifice of your best hat and scarf is better than a bitten tail.

Once the dog is safely benched, buy a catalogue and discover the whereabouts of everything, especially the position of the ring where the breed is to be judged. Comb or brush your dog sufficiently for him to make a pleasing impression on anyone who may notice him, offer him a drink and then ignore him. He will show all the better when the time comes for his class if left alone until wanted. Find out where water is available, and where there is a space set aside purposely for exercising, for it is the worst kind of offence to let a dog foul one of the empty judging rings before judging has taken place. Discover also a likely spot out of everybody's way where you can give your dog the final grooming a few minutes before he is due in the ring. At many of the big shows a special area is set apart for this purpose of final preparation; if so, find out where it is and use it. Other owners may be engaged on the same task nearby, and this is one of the occasions when a beginner with eyes open and ears pinned back can pick up a lot of useful tips.

A gentle hint may be dropped here to beginners. Don't start chatting to fellow-exhibitors when they are in the act of arriving, benching their dogs, or preparing them for the ring. We all know dog shows are holiday outings for many, and goodwill is rampant, but some preoccupation on the part of your neighbours who are just as anxious to bench their dogs sensibly as you were yours, is understandable, so you might just as well talk to yourself. Plenty of time for conversation when the serious business of the day is over, which is the judging.

Find out what time judging is billed to begin, and if you are not entered in the first of the classes keep your attention glued to the ring from the start until it is time to go and collect your exhibit. Note the judge's methods, also whether he is progressing slowly or fast, and the number of entries in the intervening classes, and thereby hazard a guess as to the approximate time you will be wanted in the ring. According to whether the classes immediately preceding yours are well filled or otherwise, fetch your dog from his bench fully a class or two before the one in which he is to appear, to give your self time for the final attention to his coat.

He should be happy to see you and display joyful anticipation at having the show collar and lead placed on him in readiness for the pleasant routine which is associated in his mind with such happenings if you have trained him properly. Maintain this cheerful outlook by praise and encouragement and take him to the selected grooming-place. Go over him very thoroughly first with a coarse comb. Any uncombed spikes of hair left under the body or inside the legs are terribly conspicuous in the ring. then effect the final touches with a brush, concluding by brushing up the leg hair in a manner calculated to present each leg to the best advantage, and persuade the facial furnishings forwards. Keep an eye and an ear trained meantime in the direction of the ring lest you are not there when wanted. Never let it be said you are one of the people who cannot be found when your class is called in. Ring-stewards sometimes walk miles in the course of a long day chasing up absent – or more accurately absent-minded – exhibitors. The judge may be the lenient sort who will hold up proceedings until all are assembled, but his task is tough enough anyway without placing such a strain upon his courtesy, so it is up to you not to be 'among the missing'.

While waiting at the ringside for the crucial moment of entering the ring, continue brushing your dog gently. This helps to steady the nerves of both dog and owner. Never allow other people to distract your attention from your dog, from the moment you fetched him off his bench until such a time as you have finished with the judging-ring for the day. When it is time for your class, lead your dog into the ring with confidence. As remarked earlier you have to possess enough of this essential quality for yourself and the dog too. And not only confidence *for* him but *in* him. The exhibitor who enters a ring thinking 'my dog won't stand a chance among this lot' is beaten before the race has begun and ten to one the dog won't try either. The ring-steward will hand you your ring-number card, which you pin to your coat where it will be easily seen while never taking your eyes off your dog. Then concentrate on your dog looking his best. Keep him happy and interested and under perfect control. Don't wander all over the ring; if in doubt where to locate yourself stand still and the steward will soon instruct you where you should be. Watch out for the behaviour and temperaments of the dogs next to you. They cannot always be trusted not to snap at your exhibit. Be jolly sure yours does not do this to them. Keep alert and watch the judge. You may have to wait a considerable time while other exhibits are being examined. Put this period to good use by cultivating the art of keeping one eye on the judge and the other on your dog. It can be acquired. While waiting your turn, or when the judge is busy at the other end of the ring, do not exhaust your own and the dog's energies by keeping it keenly at attention incessantly. No sense in wasting a wonderful show stance when nobody that matters is looking at it. The wise handler lets the dog relax at such moments. Don't perform elaborate grooming; the ring is not the place for it; but just stoop and titivate the dog a little with brush or comb, thus keeping him quiet.

Be quick off the mark, however, should the judge look your way, and be ready to have your dog smartly on its toes instantly. By this time you will have discovered the judge's methods. Most judges follow a routine of some sort. The majority prefer to see all the competititors going round the ring first, in which case be sure you have your dog moving and showing to advantage, led by your left hand and consequently on the inner side of the moving circle. Some judges prefer to handle each exhibit first and move them afterwards. Wherever you are asked to move or stand, by either the judge or the ring-steward, remember they have to be obeyed and silently. If told to stand your dog on a certain spot, go exactly where you are told, not somewhere vaguely near to it, and stay on that spot, don't keep shifting about.

The judge usually examines each dog in turn on a table. Make it easy for him by keeping your hands out of his way and remaining quite dumb until he asks you the dog's age. Answer promptly without any elaboration, and if the dog is anything under two years state the age in months. Try to keep calm all the time you are in the ring. Any agitation or nervousness on your part is conveyed immediately to your dog and is no help. When asked to move the dog, lift it down deftly and unhurriedly from the table, allowing yourself a moment to tidy with the comb or brush any part of the dogs coat which has been disarranged by the judge, and to adjust the collar so that the lead attachment is under the dog's face and not just anyhow over his ears. Then lead the dog across the full extent of the ring in a straight line away from the judge, returning in a similarly straight line back to where the judge is standing. Keep on until told to stop. It is strange how few people seem able to maintain a really straight course for their exhibit, and you may have to go up and down several times before the judge can form a fair opinion of the dog's movement. He will probably require a side view of action as well, for which you must move the dog in whatever direction he indicates and switch over the lead to the other hand when necessary so that the dog moves on the side of you nearest the judge. Move at your normal walking speed, with your whole attention concentrated on the dog, but as ever with one eye on the judge. Don't run, and don't crawl. Soundness is the most important factor in any breed, and at no time is the possession of it more apparent than when the dog is moving. Your dog may possess the most wonderful of heads, but unless he has also sound legs and feet and uses them right his head will not take him very far, for he doesn't depend on it to get himself around. Certain failings only come to light when the dog is in action. Of many a dog has it been said he looked a picture standing but lost on movement. The competent judge of a Scottish Terrier will want to see from every possible angle that the animals's movement is smooth, easy and straightforward, with free action at shoulder, stifle and hock, and suggestive of agility combined with great propelling power.

The ring applies the acid test to all your previous training, and when halted your dog should automatically come to attention with ears and tail up, watching for the rewarding bit of liver you will give him from your right-hand pocket at judicious intervals – only when deserved. Do not throw the liver to him unless you know him to be a particularly smart fieldsman and a sure catch. Hand it to him, for a piece dropped in the ring causes much unnecessary sniffing of the ground by other exhibits as well as your own. You may have accustomed him to showing his best and brightest for a ball, but it is not a popular move to bounce a ball in the ring. It may disconcert someone else's dog, especially when you inevitably lose control of it. The mere sight of it in your hand should be enough to gain the dog's attention, but a titbit is the safer plan.

When your dog is standing well, let it alone. Judges are mobile and can move into position to best see the dog. When the judge moves away do not pursue him. Others may crowd round him thrusting their dogs as they think under his notice, but this seldom pays. Since by doing so they leave more room elsewhere take advantage of it. Distance lends enchantment, and if your dog is a good one posing satisfactorily he will be better appreciated in the open space than when crushed in between the others. If the judge lines up the dogs in a particular order you have no choice but to stay in the position in which you have been placed. He has good reasons for standing you where he did, and few things are more irritating to the judge than exhibitors trying to wangle their dogs into a higher place.

Remember the other exhibitors in the ring are there for the same purpose as yourself. They, too, have paid entry fees. Show as much consideration for their chances as you expect them to show for yours. Nowhere is the old adage 'Do as you would be done by' more applicable than it is in a dog show. When the final line-up takes place accept the awards whatever they may be with equanimity. The purpose for which you have entered your dog may be threefold. If a first attempt you may view the whole business as a trial-ground for yourself and the dog, but even so most people hope to get 'in the money' by winning one or other of the usual three prizes in a class. Primarily, however, you desire an expert's opinion on your dog's merits, and indirectly you discover this by your position at the conclusion of each class. If you have entered in subsequent classes stay in the ring; even if you have been at the bottom of the previous class it is an insult to the judge to show your disappointment by fading out before your time. Incidentally, somebody has got to stand there, and if it falls to your lot do look as if you liked it. It costs less than nothing to depart looking pleased, and withering looks will not change the markings in the judge's book. The decision of the judge on the day is final, but he is only one of many. You may do better or you may do worse, on a different day under a different judge, so do not despair if you have no luck on the first outing. Bit by bit one learns what is good and how to show it to advantage.

If your dog has been placed, which means he has been either first, second, third or reserve in his class, display his prize-cards above his bench when you replace him there after the judging, and see if his water-bowl needs replenishing. Do not forget to exercise him at regular intervals if the show is of all-day duration, but he must not be away from his bench more than a few minutes at a time. The public pays to come in and admire the exhibits on their benches, and in any case nothing more surely sickens a young dog of show surroundings than to be trailed aimlessly around by its misguided owner who is afraid to let it out of his (invariably her) sight. If the usual mealtime of your dog occurs in show hours, it is to be hoped you remember to take his food along for him to enjoy on his bench plenty of time before the journey homewards.

When opportunity offers take a seat at the ringside and watch the successful, whose methods you hope to emulate. One of the most illuminating examples of clever ringcraft may sometimes be seen if a dog which has been putting up an indifferent show in the hands of a novice is taken over and handled by an expert. That its ring demeanour is promptly improved beyond belief is not magic, it is merely skilful handling acquired by experience, adaptability and much practise. The original owner may be diffident, or may be inattentive. The expert is neither. By sheer concentration and understanding of the dog's mind he conveys to it by means of the lead just what he wants it to do, at the same, time inspiring it with more confidence or calming its excitability, according to its needs. Naturally such special ability has little power with an utterly unschooled dog, but the whole point is that the connecting link between handler and dog – in other words the lead – is not unlike an electric wire, inasmuch as it conveys an invisible two-day current from one to the other. A handler of keen perceptions is conscious at once of the dog's reactions, while the dog reflects immediately whatever attitude of mind is adopted by the handler. Scottish Terriers in particular have an almost uncanny gift of sensing your moods. Any anger, irritation, anxiety or nervousness on your part is transmitted along the lead only too surely. Hence the immense importance of supplying the right stimulus from the human end; such qualities as dignity and self-possession combined with a modicum of assertiveness.

12

Judging

IN course of time the successful exhibitor may be invited to judge. Without judges there would be no dog shows. The whole system of breeding, exhibiting and dealing in dogs hangs upon their decisions. Thus the evolution of a breed is largely in their hands, and judging is a big responsibility not to be undertaken lightly. The responsibility is not to the exhibitors, nor yet to the show executive, but to the breed. As a judge, one is for the time being in a position of power, and if this power is not exercised fairly and competently much harm results.

By accepting the duties of a judge one is undertaking professional work of a kind, and must therefore possess not only extensive knowledge of the breed to be judged, but also a clear idea of a technique to be employed in the doing of it.

No one should presume to judge unless he is fully conversant with the standard of the breed. This is of the first importance. The standard provides a word-picture of an ideal dog, and the competent judge enters the ring with a clear mental ideal with which he has to compare the exhibits before him. This means he is not merely making comparisons with the best dog present on the day, but with the best imaginable. There are lamentably few dogs that conform to the standard in all particulars, and the best dog present on the day may fall very short of being a perfect specimen. But when experience and a correct interpretation of the standard enables a judge to have a picture in his mind of the ideal animal, his judging is based upon a solid foundation.

That which is the best dog of today may not be the best dog of tomorrow, for individual type changes with progress. It may change for the worse, or it may change for the better, but change it must, however slightly. But the mental ideal of correct breed type remains the same yesterday, today and forever, and though improvements in detail are added through the years, breed type does not alter. And it is that indefinable thing every good dog, however many desirable points he has in detail, should possess first and foremost. He should primarily look like a Scottish Terrier. A dog may have the longest of heads, the shortest and sturdiest of bodies and the straightest of fronts and yet not look like a Scottish Terrier because he lacks the fundamental type and the unique conformation of the breed. One frequently reads in judges' reports such phrases as 'not my type' or 'I prefer them to be so-and-so', or 'too such-and-such for my liking' and so forth. The reader of such reports may well ask by what right has any judge to entertain preferences and prejudices or to imply that he is looking for a special type of his own choosing. There is only one standard and therefore can but be only one correct type. Two judges may vary slightly in their interpretation of the standard, but it is so worded that it leaves no doubt in the mind as to what is wanted in the main essentials, and the judge who sets himself up to pretend he knows better is only demonstrating how little he knows.

Fortified and guided by a mental ideal, a judge should quickly become so absorbed in his task of concentrating on the exhibits to be judged that every other thought is banished from his mind. So utterly oblivious should he be of the identities of either the dogs or those handling them that neither the past performances of the former nor the individualities of the latter can affect his placings. A dog may have been winning at countless shows and be so well known as to be instantly recognizable, but under a conscientious judge this fact makes no difference; such a dog, by being entered for competition with others, starts level with them and should be compared and judged on his merits precisely as if he had never been seen before. As for the human element in a ring – the exhibitors – a judge who allows himself to distinguish one from another is in sorry plight. His task is greatly simplified if he views them all as mere puppets or pawns to be moved about the ring as occasion demands, but never to be recognized as anything more than necessary attendants each in control of a lead with a dog on the end of it. The very fact that dogs have to be shown on leads, depending on human guidance, lays the way open for favouritism if judges do not steel themselves against such a charge. But the added fact that each is known to the judge on the day only by a number and not by a name should be sufficient indication that the number is enough. Novice judges sometimes feel embarrassment at having to judge the dogs of people they know. They hesitate between treating their friends too well because they are their friends, or too harshly for exactly the same reason. The only cure for their indecision is to remember that a judge is for the time being in a realm apart and has no friends. He may have dozens at other times, but the surest way to lose the lot is to distinguish them one from another in the ring. To do so is to admit that he is conscious of the wrong end of the lead, to which he must deliberately blind himself.

Novice judges are not alone in their liability to fall into this trap, for there exist championship show judges of some experience who should know better who unconsciously give themselves away by such remarks as 'I make a point of encouraging the novice exhibitor', or 'I never award both Challenge Certificates to the same owner'. Both tantamount to admitting that it was not the dogs they were judging.

Every job, even the smallest, has its own technique. Method in judging dogs there must be. Before undertaking such a task, thought should be given to the method to be followed, for anyone acting in this capacity without a previously worked-out plan of procedure can come hopelessly to grief. One may decide to look for the best in a class first, by picking them out one by one as they go round the ring, and standing these aside in a corner pending closer examination. It will usually be found that first impressions hold good, and very often the ultimate winners are drawn from these which made the strongest appeal at the start. Should one of them not come up to expectations on handling, a substitute can be found from among the less appealing. Or one may work from below upwards by grouping the worst in a class first, and then temporarily dismissing them from the mind while one looks for greater merit in those left. The system may have to be varied slightly according to whether the classes are well filled or not. Whatever method one decides to follow, an opening formula adhered to shows that discrimination has begun, and evokes the confidence of exhibitors while banishing any sensation of nervousness on the part of a novice judge. It is essential to make full use of the ring, whatever its size, to keep the exhibits well spread out clear of each other so far as space allows. It is also important to make one's procedure intelligible both to the exhibitors and to ringsiders. While a judge is judging the dogs the onlookers are judging him, and they do not find it interesting to watch someone standing about dithering with indecision, nor one who rushes through the job as if he had a train to catch; nor can they see or understand what is happening if the judge allows the dogs to close in round him all in a heap or to be cluttered up in one corner of the ring while he marks his awards. Every exhibit, good or bad is deserving of the same amount of time and critical examination spent on it, movement should be assessed both from front and rear and from side views, and when the final decision is made the first four should be called out into the centre of the ring, and placed in order of merit and made to remain there until they have been given their award cards by the steward, so that all present can see exactly which are the winners.

It is well to remember when judging that coat and age are fluctuating features for which a certain amount of allowance sometimes has to be made. Some people seem totally unable to appreciate the good in a Scot if it is not in immaculate coat and trimmed according to modern fashion. But to be swayed too much by the manner of presentation or by the particular stage of coat growth at the moment, is unbalanced judging. The indeterminate judge finds a ready excuse to eliminate some of the competitors by penalizing a coat too short, or a coat too full and long, or one not trimmed to the best advantage, or one lacking furnishings. But good texture and density of coat is discernible whether its stage of growth is long or short, and its condition on the day, being of a temporary nature, should not be allowed to outweigh completely the permanent essentials of construction, such as type, bone, ribs, quarters, etc. Trimming naturally carries weight, otherwise nobody would need to trim to compete, but trimming alone does not make the dog. It is well to form the habit of looking for soundness, balance and general merit as regards conformation among the exhibits not so skilfully presented – in other words not to allow oneself to be tricked by clever hairdressing.

Age is a factor which has to be taken into consideration in such classes as Puppy, Special Puppy or Junior, for no one can expect a six-months'-old pup to possess the maturity of its twelve or eighteen-month-old rivals, and allowance should be made for its lack of size if other considerations are satisfactory. Conversely, oversize in an immature dog should be viewed with suspicion, for with all exhibits it is a judge's duty to look ahead, remembering that the winners of today may be the sires and dams of tomorrow, and in classes with an age limit this is all the more important. The puppy which looks small in a show-ring at six or seven months old may be expected to grow on. So, too, will the twelve months youngster which appears right for size at the age. There are conflicting opinions as to the desirability of awarding Challenge Certificate to puppies under twelve months. With our breed, which takes all of two years to mature fully, it is a practice greatly to be deplored.

The individual examination of each exhibit is usually made on a table, a method originally adopted by the more aged and infirm among the judges, but now universally followed. Table criticism can be quite misleading, but it is a comfortable way of overhauling each dog. The dog which handles well on the table and appears to possess many virtues in detail may prove to be unsound when moved along the ground. The final and decisive factor should always be soundness and freedom of action coupled with a confident demeanour, and the wise judge will overlook minor failings in favour of soundness first. Carriage of ears and tail, character, expression, and above all action, cannot be estimated on a table.

A knowledgeable judge will not tolerate the habit of heading and tailing while he is actually judging the dogs. If an exhibitor sees fit to squat down at dog level and calm his exhibit while the judge's attention is elsewhere that is none of his business and may quite well be in the dog's best interests, but when under the judge's immediate observations it is an objectionable practice which is suitably discouraged by judges who know their job. The novice judge will do well to assert his authority on this point at the outset. All he incurs by doing so is respect. To attempt to assess the merits and demerits of animals propped up both ends and held in position by their handlers is absurd. If a dog cannot stand on its own legs and display itself advantageously there is obviously a good deal the matter with either its conformation or its character or both, and a dog so handled is not worth considering seriously. There have occasionally been glaring examples of dogs winning first prizes which have never once throughout a class been seen standing without human support, and when asked to show their paces have slunk along with lowered tail and a frightened demeanour. Awarding a prize to such a dog does incalculable harm. However desirable it may be on points its temperament is a poor recommendation for the breed. Some handlers have the heading and tailing habit so strongly imbued in them that if asked to shift a bit along the ring they raise the dog by neck and tail and plant it again elsewhere like a wooden dummy. Small wonder such procedure arouses the contempt of the onlookers and possibly the justifiable sarcasm of the judge who may enquire if the dog has lost the use of its legs since they cannot propel it a matter of a few yards. Some exhibitors try to compromise by allowing a natural stance for the head end of their dog but using one hand to support the tail. One of the greatest all-round judges of the past, a drawer of entries if ever there was one, a man of independence of thought and action, has many a time been seen to rap across the knuckles the hand that dared to hold a tail up in the Scottish Terrier ring.

A judge who cares for the good repute of the breed will penalize judiciously any definite signs of nervousness in the exhibits. The innate reserve of the breed and a momentary shyness displayed by a young or inexperienced puppy while being handled by a stranger is understandable, and pardonable when the puppy shows well moving; but congenital nervousness is apparent at once when a dog is shown in a normal manner, and efficient judging means assessing temperament every bit as much as external qualities. With two terriers of more or less equal merit the better shower of the two should win. No high award should ever be given to a bad shower, and where heading and tailing is taboo the bad showers, if any are present, soon come to light.

A considerate judge carries out his work quietly. He does not clap his hands or drop things in order to catch a dog's expression. He is fortunate indeed if he is provided with good ring-stewards, but even bad ring-stewards are better than nothing, and can usually be persuaded to conform to the judge's wishes. These wishes, arising from his consideration for others and more particularly for the dogs, should include a preference for silence. The Kennel Club issues fairly comprehensive instructions to ring-stewards, but nowhere is it suggested that they refrain from shouting. To announce the numbers of the winners in the last class, to yell for the numbers required for the next class, and to shout out the number of the class itself – all these are totally unnecessary in a well-run show. There is an award board on which the numbers of the winners are clearly displayed for all to see, and it is up to the exhibitors to be on the spot in time for their classes. Even if they are the erring sort who have to be fetched from their benches by the steward, he does no good by shouting for them as well. Many a young exhibit has been put right off showing by the sudden loud utterance of a ring-steward making some quite unnecessary announcement, while the effect of a stentorian roar on the ear of a judge who is concentrating and probably trying to make a few notes can be distracting to say the least of it. Heaven knows the dogs themselves are capable of providing quite enough noise in a show without adding to it. A fitting quotation for ring-stewards could be 'Of every work the silent part is best'.

The conscientious judge keeps ever in his mind the original purpose of the breed, never forgetting he is judging a working terrier, in which activity, balance, proportion, muscular power, hardihood, general usefulness and a confident bearing must rank higher than a sum of excellencies in detail. If he is a breeder he may have stronger leanings towards certain features than others, but in judging he sinks all personal preferences in his primary concern for the welfare of the breed. Knowing that a virtue carried to excess constitutes a failing, he will penalize exaggerations.

13

Business

KEEPING dogs purely as a hobby demands no special business ability, but once the serious task of breeding and selling is undertaken the owner becomes to some extent a dealer. Dog-breeding and dealing can be a profitable pursuit, though to depend upon it for a livelihood (as some have to) is perforce somewhat precarious as is the case with all livestock. The attitudes of those who cause Scottish Terriers to be born into this world vary **very** much. Some view the occupation purely as a hobby with no thought of profit, and quite often when such people raise puppies they distribute them among their friends as presents. Such light-hearted approach to dog-breeding is really doing a dis-service to the dog-breeding community, for many a kennel is kept going by its sales of puppies and surplus stock, and the gift puppy robs some breeder of a possible client. Moreover, from the dog's standpoint it is bad policy ever to part with one free gratis except in very special circumstances. People seldom value that for which they have not had to pay. Every pure-bred puppy, if healthy and properly reared, has a value, and even if a merely nominal charge is made to cover the cost of rearing alone, the buyer will be more likely to appreciate the dog and take reasonable care of it.

There are others, unfortunately, who view the production of puppies purely as a commercial proposition. Not for them are any anxieties as to whether their products approach the standard or whether they will be any credit to the breed or their breeder. So long as each pup is turned into cash at the earliest possible moment they care not about repeat orders, or satisfied clients, or the after-welfare of the puppy.

The following remarks, however, are offered for the benefit of novice breeders who go in for Scottish Terriers and want to make their dog-keeping a success from every angle, including the financial. The beginner is wise if for the first few years he sells every puppy but one from each litter bred, and does so before they are three months old. The one retained should be the best bitch puppy. If it later proves a disappointment and no improvement on its dam on reaching maturity, that also is just as well sold, for it is essential to keep numbers down if a kennel is to pay its way. The resulting funds from the sale of a young litter ought if possible to cover the cost of its production and rearing, with a small credit balance in hand. For the sake of example, the stud fee may have been £20, and quite apart from time and work involved the cost of the dam's extra feeding and that of say four puppies up to eight weeks old, works out in these days to somewhere around £60, at the very least. This does not take into consideration such items as heating, lighting and cooking, which in the case of many beginners are a charge on the general household expenses. Consequently, selling three out of four pups at eight weeks old at a figure sufficient to allow a small margin of profit means that they should fetch more than £30 each. In fact, £30–£35 is a fair price for a novice breeder to ask. If he can get £40 for perhaps the most handsome pup in the litter, good luck to him. With a young litter for sale it is always a wise move to price each puppy a little differently; to offer, for instance, a £20, a £35 and a £40 pup, according to merit and early promise. But it has to be remembered the novice cannot demand as good a price as can the well-known breeder who would probably get twice as much for the same puppy. It pays the beginner better to quit most of his puppies young at a figure which is easily obtained than to be cluttered up with a lot of six-month-old youngsters eating their heads off and all needing training at the same time, just because he priced them too high at first. From about five to eight months is never an easy age for the unknown breeder to place his stock. A buyer will often ask for that age from an established kennel of repute, and give good money for it, but a young dog or bitch of similar quality and probably every bit as good as the expert's product, will not realize its true value when offered by a novice breeder. All the more reason to sell puppies young at first, until the breeder has gained some reputation for raising good ones.

Making a reputation for fair dealing and good stock takes a few years as a rule. Apart from sane general management of the dogs there are two factors which contribute to such reputation, one being showing and the other advertising. Dog shows are the shop-window of the dog-breeding fraternity. The novice probably makes a start by exhibiting the bitch he first purchased, and later tries out a home-bred puppy. If the latter gets in the money at a few shows, he has got a foot on the first rung of the ladder of success. But exhibit he must, and fairly frequently, if he wishes his kennel to prosper financially. Likewise he must advertise. Nothing else costs so much as oblivion, and unless a breeder is seen around plenty of shows, sometimes bringing out a new winner, and continually advertising whatever stock he has for disposal, he is all too soon forgotten. The weekly canine papers offer quite the best medium for advertising stock likely to be of interest to exhibitors and breeders, but to effect a quick turnover of one or two puppies as pets the unknown breeder may get response from a small advertisement in a local paper.

In advertising, it is the factual advertisement rather than the imaginative which sells the goods. Extolling the virtues while omitting to mention the faults results either in no response at all (since human nature is suspicious) or in a disillusioned buyer. The price should always be stated. Of little use wasting paper and postage writing for something you hope to acquire for fifteen guineas by the sound of it, and then find the owner asks fifty. The same adherence to truth is essential when a written description is sent in answer to an enquiry. Far better the prospective client should know in advance if he may expect a gay tail, or a softish coat, or big ears or similar minor failing in the animal he thinks of buying, than for him to get it home and discover faults about which he was not told and then harbour a grudge against the seller for evermore.

A novice should try to avoid thinking all his geese are swans. At one age or another almost every puppy bred may look like a budding champion, but a healthy dissatisfaction with one's own stock pays better in the long run than an inflated idea of its value. As one swallow does not make a summer, nor does one home-bred winner in a kennel justify that kennel's prices soaring into the heights.

When selling a puppy, it is desirable to hand over with it a brief diet sheet as a guide to the buyer. Even if the latter is an experienced owner, it lets him know to what foods the pup has been accustomed and at what hours. Further, an assurance that any queries which may arise later regarding the puppy's welfare will be dealt with and answered to the best of the seller's ability, is only another way of describing service after sales and is an aid to good business.

The best recommendations of which any kennel can boast are satisfied clients and repeat orders. If a buyer really means business he will take the trouble to call and see the dog, or arrange for some knowledgeable person to view it on his behalf. To send any dog on approval is asking for trouble, for should it be returned it can bring every sort of infection into the kennel. When selling abroad, the need for accuracy and a truthful description of every detail about the animal concerned is more than ever necessary. The overseas buyer places his trust in British veracity and honour, and counts on obtaining value for money. British breeders have a fine tradition to maintain. To betray this trust and this tradition by sending out an animal at a price exceeding its value is not only injuring the repute of British dogdom in general but is a short-sighted policy, since a buyer so treated will take good care to deal elsewhere next time. The expert trade in pedigree dogs was never so brisk as it has been since the Second World War, and Scottish Terriers of every colour and all ages are among the breeds commanding good prices and a steady market in all parts of the world. The Scot's natural adaptability and hardihood enable him to suit himself remarkably well to almost every kind of climate.

A final word of guidance to those inexperienced in dog-dealing. When a sale has resulted through the recommendation of a fellow-breeder, it is customary to pay commission on the purchase-price of the dog to the breeder who sent along the client. No matter whether it be a £10 or a £100 sale, the usual commission is ten per cent of the price. Prospective buyers who call or enquire about stock should always be asked, if they do not vouchsafe the information first, the source of their enquiry. It may be through an advertisement, or the result of admiring one's dogs at a show, or could have arisen in many different ways, but if the recommendation came from another breeder, it is but courteous and businesslike to send that breeder commission, in view of the fact that, had they been able to supply the type of dog wanted, they would themselves have effected a sale direct.

G

14

Common Ailments

SCOTTISH TERRIERS are no more prone to illness than any other breed, provided that you take care to purchase your puppy from a recognized breeder, preferably one recommended by any one of the eight Scottish Terrier Breed Clubs in Great Britain. (See appendix B).

In this way you will ensure getting, as far as humanly possible, a well bred and healthy dog of good temperament with probably quite a number of champions in its pedigree.

Dogs purchased from unknown sources may be a few pounds cheaper but the saving in cost has so often been found to disappear very quickly in veterinary surgeon's bills. This point cannot be stressed too highly to an intending purchaser of a 'Scottie' puppy – like everything else in this life it pays to buy the best and Scottish Terriers are not one of easiest of breeds to whelp and rear, hence a breeder's average costs per puppy are much higher in Scottish Terriers than in many other breeds.

Every owner of a dog should possess a clinical thermometer and be able to take the dog's temperature. Dogs that are fed, housed, groomed and exercised properly usually build up a strong resistance to disease, but on the principle of 'better be sure than sorry' it is always desirable to check up on a dog's temperature if he seems to be at all out of sorts. This is done by inserting the thermometer (previously well-smeared with Vaseline) into the dog's rectum about two-thirds of its length. Do this very gently, having someone to hold the dog standing still the while, and if there is any resistance do not apply force but alter the direction of the thermometer either upwards or downwards a little. Before inserting it make sure the mercury was shaken down to 98 degrees or below. Hold it in the rectum for over a minute, and if on reading it registers more than 101 degrees there is probably something wrong with the dog and he should be kept in, kept quiet, and under observation until his trouble, whatever it is, may be diagnosed. A dog's normal temperature is 101 degrees, with slight variations. Another indication of any deviation from good health is the state of the pulse. Every dog owner should be capable of feeling a dog's pulse. This is done by placing a finger over the artery to be found on the inside of the thigh. It takes a little practise to discover the right spot, but once found you become familiar with the feel of it. The number of beats per minute in a healthy adult Scot is normally ninety or thereabouts. Too rapid pulse may indicate the start of a feverish illness; too slow a pulse may mean heart trouble or great debility.

Other guides to a dog's condition are the gums and tongue, which should be pink and clean; the eyes, which should be bright and clear; and the nose, which should be damp and cool under most conditions. Do not expect the nose to be perpetually cold and damp, however, for when a dog is asleep or resting he not infrequently has a drying nose and not very cold one. There is a difference, however, between the temporarily dry nose (which goes wet and cold again as soon as the dog wakes up) and the crusted or hot nose which stays that way even when the dog is out and about.

If sickness is suspected, keep a check on all the above items and you may be in a position to diagnose the trouble.

A summary of the contents essential to have in the dog's miniature medicine chest is as follows:

Cottonwool	Worm tablets
Liquid paraffin	Travel sickness tablets
Olive oil	Thermometer
T.C.P.	Boric acid ointment
Dettol	Penicillin ointment
Otodex eye ointment	

There are whelping troubles, fractures, deep wounds and suchlike which call for skilled surgery, and whoever keeps a dog should be sure to know of a qualified veterinary surgeon within reach. But a daily overhaul of each dog in a kennel should ensure that the first symptoms of ill-health are noted at once, and very often if treated promptly that which could become a serious disorder may be nipped in the bud and prove nothing but a minor upset. The hints which follow refer only to troubles which may be successfully dealt with at home. The first and most important thing to remember with a dog who is at all out of sorts is to FAST him. It is Nature's own method. A sick dog does not look for food and is far better without it. Some inflammatory complaints, such as gastritis, cause undue thirst, and when the dog is observed to be drinking far more water than usual, his drinking-water must be withheld, and instead offer him a small quantity of slightly warm water, or half milk and half water, in which a teaspoonful of honey is stirred. This can sustain a dog for several days if need be, and quite often puts him right, whatever has been wrong, without any other treatment at all, provided he is allowed rest, quiet and warmth and complete starvation from all other foods. To try and tempt with food a sick dog which is disinclined to eat it is to do him much more harm than good.

Biliousness

This can take several forms most of which are caused through liver derangements. The most usual form is the bringing up of a yellow-coloured bile, often with a lot of white froth. Put the dog on a light diet (rice) for a day or two and this should stop. If you notice partly chewed bits of rough grass in the bile do not worry as the dog has merely used nature's remedy to try and cure itself.

Another form and more serious is for a dog to vomit up a whole meal. Firstly clear up the mess so that he does not try and re-eat it and then put the dog onto glucose and water for 48 hours gradually bring it back onto its usual meals via a light diet first. Any signs of continuous sickness consult your veterinary surgeon immediately.

Burns or Scalds

Apply boric acid ointment, cover with cotton wool and bandage. Replace twice a day. In an emergency, if the ointment is not to hand, sprinkle the burn freely with flour and bandage until the ointment can be obtained.

Constipation

Well kept dogs seldom suffer from this although elder dogs are sometimes bothered with it. A little liquid paraffin on their meal will usually relieve this.

Diarrhoea

This may attack dogs of all ages and for many reasons such as unsuitable food, causing indigestion, or a chill. One teaspoonful three times a day of kaolin and morphine mixture readily available from any chemist or tablets available from veterinary surgeons will usually clear this up.

If there are heavy signs of blood in the faeces take professional advice immediately.

Distemper (Hardpad & Hepatitis)

These dreaded diseases need no longer hold any fear to dog owners these days as inoculations can now be given to puppies at twelve weeks old – this inoculation is called Epivax Plus.

Ears (Canker, etc.)

There are numerous forms of ear canker, however if early treatment is started with Otodex it usually clears up in a few days. Ears should be cleaned out regularly with a piece of cotton wool in a most careful way.

Eczema

When people tell you Scottish Terriers are more addicted to this than some other breeds it is just not true. If it occurs usually the owner is to blame, probably through wrong feeding. But for this and any skin irritation treat with Exmarid obtainable at Boots and other chemists. This treatment is also suggested for mange.

Eclampsia

This is convulsions in bitches before or during whelping. It is *not* really a common complaint and usually occurs in a bitch which has insufficient calcium and vitamin D in her diet during her pregnancy.

The symptoms vary from nervousness and mild convulsions to severe attacks which may send the bitch into a coma. The veterinary surgeon must be called at once and a calcium injection given or the bitch will die.

Eyes

Occasionally a dog has discharge from the eyes. Bathe them clean, then dry and apply golden eye ointment (obtainable from the chemist) round the lids. If this does not cure it ask your veterinary surgeon for a more potent eye ointment.

Worms

Small white threadworms which are often present in puppies and brood bitches can be cured with Coopers Coopane Tablets obtainable from your veterinary surgeon. However, other forms of worms such as tapeworms must be treated by your veterinary surgeon as soon as they are noticed.

A recipe for an old-fashioned mixture which should be noted by all dog lovers is this:

The white of 1 egg.

½ gill of milk.

1 tablespoonful of glucose.

Beat these thoroughly together and add 1 teaspoonful of Brandy.

A small teaspoonful of this mixture administered every hour or so to a sick puppy that will not eat, or to a dog exhausted by illness, is the most amazing pick-me-up and veritable life-saver.

All these home remedies are usually effective in mild cases. Owners of dogs should have no hesitation in consulting their veterinary surgeon if the condition does not show signs of improvement in 24-36 hours.

A very comprehensive book on the care of your dog has been published by Popular Dogs under the title of *First-Aid and Nursing for Your Dog*. This is by F. Andrew Edgson, M.R.C.V.S. and Olwen Gwynne-Jones and deals in a very detailed manner with all the ailments owners are likely to encounter during the life of their pet.

APPENDIX A
Breed Registrations

Year	Number	Year	Number	Year	Number
1947	5,849	1957	1,418	1967	1,514
1948	4,550	1958	1,483	1968	1,576
1949	3,961	1959	1,482	1969	1,505
1950	3,018	1960	1,448	1970	1,614
1951	2,610	1961	1,395	1971	1,273
1952	1,866	1962	1,485	1972	1,554
1953	1,665	1963	1,338	1973	1,356
1954	1,519	1964	1,523	1974	1,302
1955	1,440	1965	1,449	1975	1,176
1956	1,587	1966	1,435		

APPENDIX B
Breed Clubs
U.K. Clubs and their Secretaries, as at July 1976*

DURHAM AND NORTHUMBERLAND SCOTTISH TERRIER CLUB
Mrs. M. A. Walton, 187 Brierton Lane, Hartlepool, Cleveland.

NORTH MIDLANDS SCOTTISH TERRIER CLUB
Miss S. M. Harrold, 134 Old Road, Chesterfield, Derbyshire S40 3QP.

NORTH OF ENGLAND SCOTTISH TERRIER CLUB
Mrs. V. Sadler, Marleen Cottage, Glen Road, Whatstandwell,
   Derbyshire DE4 5EH.

SCOTTISH TERRIER BREEDERS AND EXHIBITORS ASSOCIATION
Mr. P. Cockrill, Hampstead Norreys, Newbury, Berks RG16 0TT.

SCOTTISH TERRIER CLUB (ENGLAND)
Mrs. F. Wright, 7 Cherry Garth, Lund, Nr. Driffield, Yorks YO25 9TD.

SCOTTISH TERRIER CLUB (SCOTLAND)
Dr. L. Rosenbloom, 23 Buckingham Terrace, Edinburgh EH4 3RE.

SOUTH WALES AND MONMOUTHSHIRE SCOTTISH TERRIER CLUB
Mrs. F. M. Sheppard, Keepers Lodge, Llansannor, Cowbridge,
   Glamorgan CF7 7RX.

ULSTER SCOTTISH TERRIER CLUB
Mrs. E. Simpson, Penniclea House, Ballykell, Dromore, Co. Down,
   N. Ireland.

WEST OF ENGLAND SCOTTISH TERRIER CLUB
Mrs. A. V. Richardson, Ashley Lodge, Box, Chippenham,
   Wiltshire SN14 9AN.

*The names and addresses of current secretaries of any club can always be
obtained from the Kennel Club, 1 Clarges Street, Piccadilly, London
   W1Y 8AB (Telephone 01-493 6651).

Overseas Clubs

UNITED STATES OF AMERICA
Scottish Terrier Club of America
with the following regional clubs:
Scottish Terrier Club of California
Washington State Scottish Terrier Club
Scottish Terrier Club of Greater Washington D.C.
Scottish Terrier Club of New England
Scottish Terrier Club of Western Virginia
Scottish Terrier Club of Greater Miami, Inc.
Scottish Terrier Club of Chicago
Scottish Terrier Club of Northern Ohio
Scottish Terrier Club of Michigan
Heart of America Scottish Terrier Club
Scottish Terrier Club of Greater Houston
Scottish Terrier Club of Greater Atlanta
Scottish Terrier Club of Greater New York
Scottish Terrier Club of Greater Dayton
Scottish Terrier Club of Long Island
Scottish Terrier Club of Greater Baltimore Area
The Greater Dallas Scottish Terrier Club
Aloha Scottish Terrier Club
San Francisco Bay Scottish Terrier Club
The Phoenix Scottish Terrier Club
Oregon Scottish Terrier Club
Jacksonville Area Scottish Terrier Club
Top O' The World Scottish Terrier Club (Alaska)

AUSTRALIA
Scottish Terrier Club (Australia) of New South Wales
Scottish Terrier Club of Queensland
Scottish Terrier Club of Victoria

CANADA
Scottish Terrier Club of Canada
Scottish Terrier section of the British Columbia All Terrier Club

SOUTH AFRICA
Scottish Terrier Section of the Shortlegged Terrier Club of South Africa

SWEDEN
Skotte – Federationen

The current addresses of the secretaries of any of the above clubs are available from the honorary secretary of the Scottish Terrier Breeders' and Exhibitors' Association, England.

APPENDIX C

Champions 1960–1975

Name	Sex	Birth	Sire	Dam	Breeder	Owner
1960						
Allascot Clover	B	27.9.57	Ch. Glenview Sir Galahad	Allascot Amber	Major J. Howard	Major J. Howard
Broadeaves Briar Rose	B	29.12.58	Glengordon Greensleeves	Reanda Rochelle of Broadeaves	Miss D. M. White	Miss D. M. White
Caldicot Meg O' Marine	B	31.7.57	Ammanview Alistair	Brema Bonnie	Mr. G. Kavanagh	Mr. L. Burston
Darmar Will I Do	D	10.8.58	Ch. Bardene Boy Blue	Darmar About Time	Major and Mrs. F. Darroch & Mr. H. Wright	Mr. M. Andoh
Desco Daphne	B	15.2.59	Ch. Happy Kimbo	Desco Daylight	Mrs. L. J. Dewar	Mrs. L. J. Dewar
Grand Revel of Hadlow	B	20.6.58	Ch. Greeba Hawesgarth Robin	Lady Guinevere of Hadlow	Miss S. V. Pollock	Mr. D. Holman
Jokyl Here We Go	D	7.11.58	Ch. Reanda Rohan	Eilburn Elwyn	Mr. M. Punton	Mr. G. Jackson
Kennelgarth Great Scot	D	11.8.57	Kennelgarth Tweedledee	Ch. Kennelgarth Gleam	Miss B. Penn Bull	Miss B. Penn Bull
Penvale Persuader	B	3.6.59	Balgownie Bix	Brienbry Butterkisk	Mr. J. Jeffs	Mr. R. A. Knapp
Reanda Luna Rossa	B	9.4.58	Ch. Greeba Hawesworth Robin	Ch. Reanda Ria Bella	Mrs. E. Meyer	Mr. M. Akizawa
1961						
Bardene Black Jewel	B	10.7.60	Ryeland Regal Scot	Bardene Blue Cap	Mr. G. Young	Mr. & Mrs. A. Stamn

Name	Sex	Birth	Sire	Dam	Breeder	Owner
Glenview Merry Princess	B	8.7.59	Glenview Rocket	Ch. Glenview Princess	Mr. A. H. Gee	Mr. A. H. Gee
Hardlyn Rufus	D	17.11.58	Ch. Reanda Rohan	Hardlyn Rosita	Mrs. V. G. Hardy	Mrs. V. G. Hardy
Kennelgarth Eros	D	14.4.57	Ch. Viewpark Vincent	Ch. Kennelgarth Venus	Miss B. Penn Bull	Miss B. Penn Bull
Kennelgarth Viking	D	20.11.59	Ch. Kennelgarth Eros	Ch. Kennelgarth Gleam	Miss B. Penn Bull	Miss B. Penn Bull
Kentwelle Krocus	B	22.12.59	Ch. Greeba Hawesgarth Robin	Kentwelle Kristie	Mrs. Y. M. Upex	Mrs. E. Meyer
Niddbank Kirsty	B	18.9.59	Niddbank Headline	Niddbank Prudence	Mrs. K. M. Ross	Mr. P. Cunningham
Reanda Gloxinia of Hadlow	B	7.4.59	Ch. Glenview Sir Galahad	Ch. Lady Meg of Hadlow	Miss S. V. Pollock	Mrs. E. Meyer
Reanda Reeba	B	10.11.59	Reanda Blackamoor	Reanda Ruta	Mrs. E. Meyer	Mrs. W. M. Robertson
Reanda Rexis	D	19.9.59	Ch. Reanda Ribot	Ch. Reanda Silver Belle	Mrs. E. Meyer	Mrs. E. Meyer
Viewpark Dictator	D	23.7.59	Ch. Greeba Hawesgarth Robin	Valencia Queen	Mr. A. N. MacLaren	Mrs. A. C. Ayer
1962 Bardene Bartelo	B	11.5.61	Ryeland Raffie	Bardene Breezandi	Mr. W. Palethorpe	Mr. W. Palethorpe
Bardene Bingo	D	28.6.61	Bardene Blue Starlite	Bardene Blue Cap	Mr. G. Young	Mr. E. H. Stuart
Cumnock Clansman	D	12.1.60	Ch. Kennelgarth Eros	Ch. Cumnoch Sonnet	Miss B. D. Sedorski	Miss B. D. Sedorski

Name	Sex	Date	Sire	Dam	Breeder	Owner
Gaywyn Viscountess	B	16.2.61	Ch. Kennelgarth Viking	Gaywyn Countess	Mrs. M. Owen	Mrs. M. Owen
Glenview Golden Disc	D	16.9.60	Glenview Guardian	Glenview Cindy	Mr. A. H. Gee	Mr. A. H. Gee
Reanda Cellan of Conett	D	1.6.58	Ch. Cool of Conett	Curtis of Conett	Mr. A. R. Hanson	Mr. F. W. Fraser
Reanda Kentwelle Kingpin	D	28.7.58	Ch. Reanda Roger Rough	Kentwelle Kamelia	Mrs. Y. M. Upex	Mrs. E. Meyer
Reanda Rexana	B	12.10.60	Ch. Reanda Rexis	Ch. Reanda Luna Rossa	Mrs. E. Meyer	Mrs. E. Meyer
Reanda Roumelia	B	11.4.57	Ch. Reanda Rohan	Ch. Reanda Runic Regal	Mrs. E. Meyer	Mrs. J. Hepburn
Scotvale Soraya	B	23.5.59	Wyrebury Worthy	Scotvale Sandra	Mr. H. Heaton	Mr. A. B. Movie
Woodmansey Winetaster	D	29.9.60	Wyrebury Worthy	Woodmansey Wanderlust	Mr. H. Wright	Mr. H. Wright
Nedwar Balgownie Betula	B	30.1.60	Maigarth Marantic	Balgownie Bairn	Mr. A. Black	Mr. R. Ashworth
1963 Eskside Dainty Lady	B	8.9.59	Maigarth Mahthappen	Eilburn Rohanna	Mrs. M. Punton	Mr. A. Meston
Gaywyn Bonnilass	B	16.4.62	Ch. Kennelgarth Viking	Gaywyn Bonigen	Mrs. M. Owen	Mrs. M. Owen
Gillsie Principal Girl	B	2.8.62	Ch. Bardene Bingo	Balgownie Butterfluff	Mr. W. Gill & Mr. J. McShane	Mr. W. Gill
Glenview Silver Gilt	D	7.3.61	Turfield Buckwheat	Glenview Silvernob	Mr. A. H. Gee	Mr. A. H. Gee
Kennelgarth Minerva	B	9.12.59	Kennelgarth Jupiter	Ravensden Rizzio	Mrs. M. E. Lowden	Miss B. Penn Bull

Name	Sex	Birth	Sire	Dam	Breeder	Owner
Kennelgarth Sharon	B	15.9.59	Kennelgarth Lance	Kennelgarth Sheena	Miss B. Penn Bull	Miss B. Penn Bull
Wirescot Penny	B	4.7.61	Ch. Kennelgarth Eros	Manorcourt May Sonnet	Mr. A. C. Penny	Mr. W. Bush
1964 Bardene Bemine	B	4.11.62	Ch. Bardene Eingo	Bardene Barefoot Contessa	Mr. W. Palethorpe	Mr. W. Palethorpe
Brackencroft Rye and Dry	B	26.7.62	Ch. Kennelgarth Viking	Brackenscroft Hazel Honey	Mr. C. E. Brackstone	Miss K. Boyes
Brunnoch Rapid Riser of Hadlow	B	24.7.58	Ch. Reanda Roger Rough	Ch. Glenview Lady Grace of Hadlow	Miss S. B. Pollock	Mrs. E. King
Caldicot Arabis	B	20.12.61	Caldicot Pennant	Ch. Caldicot Meg O'Marine	Mr. L. Burston	Mr. L. Burston
Comely My Hazel	B	1.4.63	Ch. Kennelgarth Viking	Brackenscroft Hazel Honey	Mr. C. E. Brackstone	Miss C. Stevenson
Gaywyn Matador	D	7.10.61	Cumnoch Kilts-a-Swinging	Gaywyn Cresta	Mrs. M. Owen	Mrs. A. Ashenden
Gaywyn Titania	B	13.8.63	Ch. Bardene Bingo	Ch. Gaywyn Viscountess	Mrs. M. Owen	Mrs. M. Owen
Glenellen Clan-Crest	D	7.9.62	Ch. Reanda Kentwell Kingpin	Reanda Rhodanthe	Mr. J. Chapman & Mr. H. McCormack	Mr. G. M. Barr
Inverdruie Scorchin	D	25.5.62	Ch. Kennelgarth Viking	Inverdruie Sparkler	Miss L. Vassilopulo	Miss C. Stevenson
Milward Meadowmist	D	29.10.62	Eckersley Yellowhammer	Milward Meadowsweet	Mrs. G. D. Yates	Mrs. G. D. Yates

Penvale Prolific	D	18.1.61	Balgownie Bix	Brienby Butterkisk	Mr. J. Jeffs	Mrs. Y. Grover Williams
Reanda the Rock	D	2.7.62	Ch. Reanda Kentwelle Kingpin	Ch. Reanda Gloxinia of Hadlow	Mrs. E. Meyer	Mrs. M. Akizawa
Walsing Winter Weather	B	3.4.60	Ch . Walsing Wild Winter	St. Quivox Quality Street	Mr. W. M. Singleton	Mr. W. M. Singleton
1965 Brio Cabin Boy	D	20.2.64	Ch. Kennelgarth Viking	Brio Chorus Girl	Miss J. Miller	Miss J. Miller
Brio Wishbone	B	20.2.64	Ch. Kennelgarth Viking	Brio Chorus Girl	Miss J. Miller	Miss J. Miller
Gaywyn Castanet	B	23.4.63	Ch. Kennelgarth Viking	Gaywyn Conchita	Mrs. M. Owen	Mrs. M. Owen
Gaywyn Emperor	D	27.8.62	Ch. Bardene Bingo	Ch. Gaywyn Viscountess	Mrs. M. Owen	Mrs. M. Owen
Gillsie Highland Lass	B	17.2.64	Ch. Kennelgarth Viking	Ch. Gillsie Principal Girl	Mr. W. Gill & Mr. J. McShane	Mr. A. Gill
Gillsie Starturn	D	17.2.64	Ch. Kennelgarth Viking	Ch. Gillsie Principal Girl	Mr. W. Gill & Mr. J. McShane	Mr. W. Gill
Gosmore Gillsie Scotch Mist	B	17.2.64	Ch. Kennelgarth Viking	Ch. Gillsie Principal Girl	Mr. W. Gill & Mr. J. McShane	Mrs. A. B. Dallison
Gregorach Glorious Twelfth	B	12.8.63	Ch. Woodmansey Winetaster	Gregorach Chequers	Miss P. Drummond	Miss P. Drummond
Kennelgarth Valorous	D	27.9.62	Ch. Kennelgarth Viking	Kennelgarth Dairymaid	Miss B. Penn Bull	Miss B. Penn Bull

Name	Sex	Birth	Sire	Dam	Breeder	Owner
Reanda Renita	B	29.4.63	Ch. Reanda Kentwelle Kingpin	Ch. Reanda Rosalina	Mrs. E. Meyer	Mrs. E. Meyer
Reanda Ringold	D	28.1.64	Ch. Bardene Bingo	Stedplane Reanda Rainette	Mrs. E. Plane	Mrs. E. Meyer
Viewpark Viking	D	18.9.63	Viewpark Red Hackle	Viewpark Fancy Fair	Mr. A. N. MacLaren	Mr. C. Rickel
1966 Bardene Bo Diddly	D	20.5.65	Bardene Blue Steptoe	Ch. Bardene Bemine	Mr. W. Palethorpe	Mr. J. Storr
Brio Pick Pocket	D	27.4.65	Ch. Kennelgarth Viking	Ch. Brio Chorus Girl	Miss J. Miller	Mrs. B. Westerstom
Eilburn Elegance	B	10.10.64	Inverdruie Scorchin	Bardene Betwixt	Mrs. M. Punton	Mrs. M. Punton
Gaywyn Bonetta	B	16.4.62	Ch. Kennelgarth Viking	Gaywyn Bonigen	Mrs. M. Owen	Mrs. M. Owen
Glenecker Golden Girl	B	13.3.65	Ch. Glenview Silver Gilt	Glenecker Silver Hammer	Mrs. M. A. Micklethwaite	Mrs. M. A. Micklethwaite
Gosmore Gillsie Scotch Lad	D	26.2.65	Ch. Kennelgarth Viking	Ch. Gillsie Principal Girl	Mr. W. Gill & Mr. J. McShane	Mr. F. Fraser
Gosmore Gillsie Scotch Lass	B	26.2.65	Ch. Kennelgarth Viking	Ch. Gillsie Principal Girl	Mr. W. Gill & Mr. J. McShane	Miss L. Stella
1967 Brio Enchantress	B	27.4.65	Ch. Kennelgarth Viking	Brio Chorus Girl	Miss J. Miller	Miss J. Miller

Name	Sex	Date	Sire	Dam	Breeder	Owner
Gaywyn Matico	B	21.4.65	Ch. Gaywyn Emperor	Gaywyn Matilda	Mrs. M. Owen	Mrs. D. Standen
Gaywyn Teasel	B	7.3.65	Ch. Gaywyn Matador	Ch. Gaywyn Titania	Mrs. M. Owen	Mrs. M. Owen
Gosmore Eilburn Admaration	D	11.11.65	Ch. Kennelgarth Viking	Bardene Betwixt	Mrs. M. Punton	Mr. & Mrs. C. Pillsbury
Kennelgarth Black Diamond	B	15.9.65	Ch. Kennelgarth Viking	Kennelgarth Dairymaid	Miss B. Penn Bull	Miss B. Penn Bull
Viewpark Truely Fair	B	17.7.66	Viewpark Dalblane March Chestnut	Viewpark Volo	Mr. A. N. MacLaren	Mr. A. N. MacLaren
1968 Brio Checkmate	D	27.6.66	Ch. Kennelgarth Eros	Ch. Brio Wishbone	Miss J. Miller	Miss J. Miller
Brio Jezebel	B	7.1.67	Kennelgarth Confucius	Brio Witchcraft	Miss J. Miller	Miss J. Miller
Gosmore Eilburn Miss Hopeful	D	12.11.66	Inverdruie Scorchin	Barden Betwixt	Mrs. M. Punton	Mrs. A. B. Dallison
Gosmore Gillson Highland King	D	4.10.66	Bardene Blue Steptoe	Ch. Gillsie Highland Lass	Mr. & Mrs. A. Gill	Mrs. A. B. Dallison
Kennelgarth Knight Errant	D	4.3.66	Ch. Kennelgarth Viking	Bardene Bingotessa	Mrs. J. Knight-Hepburn	Miss B. Penn Bull
Niddbank Nicefella	D	29.3.67	Bardene Blue Steptoe	Niddbank Nice-Un	Mr. & Mrs. J. R. Ross	Mrs. B. Hobson
Noonsun Pride	D	27.2.64	Niddbank Woodpecker of Worton	Honey Glow	Mrs. E. Perry	Mrs. N. Holland

Name	Sex	Birth	Sire	Dam	Breeder	Owner
Rodeon Rina	B	29.11.66	Gaywyn Zak	Rodeon Rosemary	Mr. H. Hughes	Mr. H. Hughes
Woodmansey Warrior	D	14.8.64	Ch. Woodmansey Winetaster	Ch. Grand Revel of Hadlow	Mr. H. Wright	Mr. H. Wright
1969						
Eilburn High Society	D	10.7.68	Ch. Inverdruie Scorchin	Bardene Betwixt	Mrs. M. Punton	Mrs. M. Punton
Eilburn Wonder Girl	B	1.6.67	Ch. Kennelgarth Viking	Bardene Betwixt	Mrs. M. Punton	Mr. Lee G. Lowe
Glenecker Golden Nob	D	26.8.66	Glenecker Foxhunter	Glenecker Glenview Glamis	Mrs. M. A. Micklethwaite	Mrs. M. A. Micklethwaite
Gosmore Eilburn Royal Lady	B	12.11.66	Ch. Inverdruie Scorchin	Bardene Betwixt	Mrs. M. Punton	Mrs. A. B. Dallison
Tambrae Tura	B	17.9.67	Ch. Gosmore Eilburn Admaration	Ch. Gaywyn Matico	Mrs. D. Standen	Mrs. D. Standen
1970						
Aberscot Gillsie Eavoy	D	23.9.68	Ch. Gosmore Eilburn Admaration	Ch. Gillsie Highland Lass	Mr. & Mrs. W. Gill	Mr. & Mrs. M. Gaskell
Aberscot Gillson Celebrity	B	25.9.67	Ch. Gosmore Eilburn Admaration	Ch. Gillsie Highland Lass	Mr. A. Gill	Mrs. Mieko Kitano
Brio Musical Box	B	2.4.68	Ch. Gosmore Eilburn Admaration	Ch. Brio Enchantress	Miss J. Miller	Miss J. Miller
Cynon Crackerjack	D	6.12.67	Caldicot Gillsie Highlander	Cynon Black Diamond	Mr. M. Lewis	Mr. M. Lewis

Name		Date	Sire	Dam		
Gaywyn Kingson	D	14.4.68	Ch. Gosmore Gillson Highland King	Ch. Gaywyn Bonetta	Mrs. M. Owen	Mrs. M. Owen
Gaywyn Lisa	B	14.4.68	Ch. Gosmore Gillson Highland King	Ch. Gaywyn Bonetta	Mrs. M Owen	Mrs. M. Owen
Tambrae Kandy	B	19.8.68	Tambrae Turpin	Tambrae Kate	Mrs. D. Standen	Mrs. D. Standen
Viewpark Amanda	B	27.6.69	Viewpark Matador	Ch. Viewpark Truely Fair	Mr. A. N. Maclaren	Mr. A. N. Maclaren
1971 Aberscot Gillsie Counsellor	D	20.1.70	Ch. Aberscot Gillsie Envoy	Ch. Gillsie Principal Girl	Mr. W. Gill	Mr. & Mrs. P. Hagezulabak
Eros Scot Black Ensign	D	11.11.65	Kennelgarth Taurus	Clynebury Castor Sugar	Mrs. H. Davies	Mr. F. J. Backham
Gillson Grandiloquence	D	25.9.67	Ch. Gosmore Eilburn Admaration	Ch. Gillsie Highland Lass	Mr. & Mrs. A. Gill	Mr. A. Gill
Gillson Serenade	B	25.9.67	Ch. Gosmore Eilburn Admaration	Ch. Gillsie Highland Lass	Mr. & Mrs. A. Gill	Mr. & Mrs. M. Gaskell
Tanbrae Tabitha	B	7.6.68	Inverdruie Scorchin	Gaywyn Keynote	Mrs. D. Standen	Mrs. D. Standen
Vox Humana of Tadwick	B	14.10.68	Bathwick Boreas	Marguerite of Agbrigg	Mr. R. W. Morris	Mrs. F. M. Sheppard
Eilburn Elite	B	10.9.67	Ch. Gosmore Admaration	Ch. Eilburn Elegance	Owner	Mrs. M. Punton
Roxeth Musidora	B	31.7.68	Glengordon Tam O'Shanter	Broadeaves Buttercup	Miss D. M. White	Mrs. L. T. Norman
Jetscot Valda	B	31.3.68	Ch. Kennelgarth Valorous	Jetscot Merle	Mrs. K. Smead	Mrs. K. Smead

Name	Sex	Birth	Sire	Dam	Breeder	Owner
1972 Gaywyn Rampage	D	8.3.70	Ch. Gaywyn Top Hat	Ch. Rodeon Rina	Mr. H. Hughes	Mrs. Muller Kok
Gaywyn Top Hat	D	24.6.68	Ch. Kennelgarth Viking	Ch. Gaywyn Teasel	Mrs. M. Owen	Mrs. M. Owen
Gillson Dublay Darcy	D	5.9.70	Ch. Gillson Grandiloquence	Dublay Chitty Bang Bang	Mr. & Mrs. B. Askin	Atsuko Koyama
Gillson Dublay Wild Enchantress	B	5.9.70	Ch. Gillson Grandiloquence	Dublay Chitty Bang Bang	Mr. & Mrs. B. Askin	Mrs. Michiko Akizawa
Glenview Fancy Lad	D	28.6.69	Glenecker Foxhunter	Glenview Fancy Free	Mr. A. H. Gee	Mrs. M. A. Micklethwaite
Jetstorm Black Magic	B	21.1.70	Ch. Gillson Grandiloquence	Jetstorm Princess	Mrs. P. Sutherland	Miss Ulla Bak
Kennelgarth I'm a Tiger	D	14.1.71	Kennelgarth Conspirator	Berwyn Ballerina	Mr. D. Colwell	Mr. Bert Malmkvuist
Kennelgarth King of Scots	D	24.6.68	Ch. Kennelgarth Viking	Ch. Gaywyn Teasel	Mrs. M. Owen	Miss B. Penn Bull
Mandavil Morning Mist	B	29.8.70	Bardene Blue Steptoe	Mandavil Merewyn	Mr. & Mrs. N. W. Manners	Mr. & Mrs. N. W. Manners
Mayson Tommy Toff	D	10.4.71	Ch. Gaywyn Kingson	Mayson Molly Toff	Mr. J. S. & Mrs. M. Gaskell	Mrs. I. Marius
Tambrae Kathe	B	6.6.70	Tambrae Turpin	Tambrae Kate	Mrs. O. Cockrill	Madame J. Sainctelette
Viewpark Anna	B	11.8.71	Ch. Viewpark Matador	Ch. Viewpark Truely Fair	Mr. A. N. Maclaren	Mr. J. and Mrs. P. Suyeter

Name	Sex	Date	Sire	Dam	Breeder	Owner
Aberscot Gillsie Bon Accord	D	20.1.70	Ch. Aberscot Gillsie Envoy	Ch. Gillsie Principal Girl	Mr. W. Gill	Mr. & Mrs. I. Fraser
1973 Brio Fair 'N Square	D	15.11.71	Ch. Brio Cabin Boy	Ch. Brio Call Me Madam	Miss J. Miller	Miss J. Miller
Gaywyn Leila	B	26.3.70	Ch. Gaywyn Emperor	Ch. Gaywyn Lisa	Mrs. M. Owen	Mrs. M. Owen
Gaywyn Wicked Lady	B	23.11.70	Ch. Gaywyn Kingson	Ch. Gosmore Eilburn Royal Lady	Mrs. A. B. Dallison	Mrs. M. Owen
Gillson Precious Gem	B	9.3.72	Ch. Gillson Grandiloquence	Gillson Serene	Mr. A. Gill	Mr. & Mrs. I. Southwick
Glenecker Jeremy Whu	D	1.3.71	Brio Jolly Miller	Glenecker Gin	Mrs. M. A. Micklethwaite	Mrs. M. A. Micklethwaite
Jetscot Viceroy	D	4.2.71	Ch. Kennelgarth King of Scots	Ch. Jetscot Valda	Mrs. K. Smead	Miss C. Jarvis
Viewpark Dana	B	17.5.72	Aberscot Acquisition	Viewpark Mayfair	Mr. A. N. Maclaren	Mr. A. N. Maclaren
1974 Boswell Bodicea	B	10.10.71	Dalblane Maestro Superb	Boswell Bit O' Luck	Mr. & Mrs. R. A. Bowles	Mr. & Mrs. R. A. Bowles
Brio Call Me Madam	B	25.9.70	Ch. Gaywyn Emperor	Ch. Brio Musical Box	Miss J. Miller	Miss J. Miller
Brio Sound of Music	B	25.9.70	Ch. Gaywyn Emperor	Ch. Brio Musical Box	Miss J. Miller	Mrs. Vanoni
Gaywyn Joel	D	23.11.71	Ch. Gaywyn Emperor	Gaywyn Busybody	Mrs. M. Owen	Mrs. M. Owen

Name	Sex	Birth	Sire	Dam	Breeder	Owner
Gaywyn Landlord	D	7.10.73	Ch. Brio Fair 'N Square	Ch. Gaywyn Leila	Mrs. M. Owen	Mrs. Muller-Kok
Jetstorm Black Mystery	B	28.3.71	Ch. Gillson Grandiloquence	Jetstorm Princess	Mrs. P. Sutherland	Mrs. E. Clerc
Kennelgarth King of Diamonds	D	17.3.72	Ch. Kennelgarth King of Scots	Ch. Kennelgarth Black Diamond	Miss B. Penn Bull	Miss B. Penn Bull
Prix Noire of Perlor	B	17.2.73	Ch. Gillson Grandiloquence	Christina of Dunsville	Mrs. Bostock	Mr. W. G. & Miss L. Hall
Reanda Rocksilver	D	5.9.72	Reanda Rock Roi	Reanda Ryeberry	Mrs. E. Meyer	Mr. & Mrs. J. McClosky
Viewpark Vanity Maid	B	1.3.73	Viewpark Matador	Ch. Viewpark Truely Fair	Mr. A. N. Maclaren	Mr. A. N. Maclaren
Woodmansey Gosmore Royal King	D	23.11.70	Ch. Gaywyn Kingson	Ch. Gosmore Eilburn Royal Lady	Mrs. A. B. Dallison	Mr. H. Wright
Gaywyn Megan	B	18.3.72	Ch. Gaywyn Top Hat	Gaywyn Modern Millie	Owner	Mrs. M. Owen
1975 Gaywyn Likely Lad	D	7.10.73	Ch. Brio Fair 'N Square	Ch. Gaywyn Leila	Mrs. M. Owen	Mrs. M. Owen
Law Lord of Scarista	D	29.4.73	Aberscot Acquisition	Ch. Aberscot Gillson Celebrity	Mr. I. Fraser	Mr. J. Falconer
Tiddlymount Royal of Jetscot	B	12.10.73	Ch. Jetscot Viceroy	Tiddlymount Kathe	Mr. J. P. & Miss V. E. Dodgson	Mrs. K. Smead
Kennelgarth Deborah	B	23.1.73	Kennelgarth Conspirator	Kennelgarth Delilah	Owner	Miss B. Penn Bull
Tiddlymount Tipple of Jetscot	B	12.10.73	Ch. Jetscot Viceroy	Tiddly-Mount Kathe	Mr. J. P. & Miss V. E. Dodgson	Mrs. K. Smead

APPENDIX D

AMERICAN KENNEL CLUB BREED STANDARD
Adopted April 1947

SKULL – (5 Points): Long, of medium width, slightly domed and covered with short hard hair. It should not be quite flat, as there should be a slight stop or drop between the eyes.

(1) MUZZLE – (5 Points): In proportion to the length of skull, with not too much taper toward the nose. Nose should be black and of good size. The jaws should be level and square. The nose projects somewhat over the mouth, giving the impression that the upper jaw is longer than the lower. The teeth should be evenly placed, having a scissors or level bite, with the former being preferable.

EYES – (5 Points): Set wide apart, small and of almond shape, not round. Color to be dark brown or nearly black. To be bright, piercing and set well under the brow.

EARS – (10 Points): Small, prick, set well up on the skull, rather pointed but not cut. The hair on them should be short and velvety.

NECK – (5 Points): Moderately short, thick and muscular, strongly set on sloping shoulders, but not so short as to appear clumsy.

CHEST – (5 Points): Broad and very deep, well let down between the forelegs.

BODY – (15 points): Moderately short and well ribbed up with strong loin, deep flanks and very muscular hindquarters.

(2) LEGS AND FEET – (10 Points): Both fore and hind legs should be short and very heavy in bone in proportion to the size of the dog. Fore legs straight or slightly bent with elbows, close to the body. Scottish Terriers should not be out at the elbows. Stifles should be well bent and legs straight from hock to heel. Thighs very muscular. Feet round and thick with strong nails, fore feet larger than the hind feet.

NOTE: The gait of the Scottish Terrier is peculiarly its own and is very characteristic of the breed. It is not the square trot or walk that is desirable in the long-legged breeds. The fore legs do not move in exact parallel planes – rather in reaching out incline slightly inward. This is due to the shortness of leg and width of chest. The action of the rear legs should be square and true and at the trot both the hocks and stifles should be flexed with a vigorous motion.

TAIL – (2½ Points): Never cut and about seven inches long, carried with a slight curve but not over the back.

COAT – (15 Points): Rather, short, about two inches, dense undercoat with outercoat intensely hard and wiry.

(3) SIZE AND WEIGHT – (10 Points): Equal consideration must be given to height, length of back and weight. Height at shoulder for either sex should be about 10″. Generally, a well balanced Scottish Terrier dog of correct size should weigh from 19 to 22 lbs. and a bitch from 18 to 21 lbs. The principal objective must be symmetry and balance.

COLOR – (2½ Points): Steel or iron grey, brindle or grizzled, black, sandy or wheaten. White markings are objectionable and can be allowed only on the chest and that to a slight extent only.

GENERAL APPEARANCE – (10 Points): The face should wear a keen sharp and active expression. Both head and tail should be carried well up. The dog should look very compact, well muscled and powerful, giving the impression of immense power in a small size.

(4) PENALTIES – Soft coat, round or very light eye, over or undershot jaw, obviously over or under size, shyness, timidity or failure to show with head and tail up are faults to be penalized. No judge should put to Winners or Best of Breed any Scottish Terrier not showing real Terrier character in the ring.

SCALE OF POINTS (For Judging at Dog Shows)

Skull 5	Neck 5	Tail 2½
Muzzle 5	Chest 5	Coat 15
Eyes 5	Body 15	Size............ 10
Ears 10	Legs and Feet 10	Color 2½
		Appearance...... 10
		Total...... 100 Pts.

BIBLIOGRAPHY

Ash, E. C. *The Scottish Terrier*, London, 1936.

Buckley, H., *The Scottish Terrier*, London, 1913.

Caspersz, D. S., *Scottish Terrier Pedigrees*, Henley-on-Thames, 1930.

—, *The Scottish Terrier*, Our Dogs, 1938.

—, *Scottish Terrier Pedigrees*, Henley-on-Thames, 1934.

—, *The Scottish Terrier Handbook*, Nicholson & Watson, London, 1951.

—, *Scottish Terrier Pedigrees. First Supplement*, Henley-on-Thames, 1951.

—, *The Scottish Terrier*, W. & G. Foyle, London, 1958.

—, *Scottish Terrier Pedigrees. Second Supplement*, Henley-on-Thames, 1962.

Davies, C. J., *The Scottish Terrier*, London, 1906.

Ewing, F. C., *The Book of the Scottish Terrier*, New York, 1932. Revised edition, 1936.

Gabriel, D., *The Scottish Terrier*, London, 1928. Second edition, 1934.

Haynes, W., *Scottish and Irish Terriers*, New York, 1912.

Johns, R., *Our Friend the Scottish Terrier*, London, 1932.

Kipling, R., *The Supplication of the Black Aberdeen*, London, 1931.

Maxtee, J., *Scotch and Irish Terriers*, London, 1909.

McCandlish, W. L., *The Scottish Terrier*, Our Dogs, 1909.

Scottish Terrier Club of America Year Book, (1965).

INDEX

Selecting a stud dog, 110
Selling, 174
Setting Sun, 44
Shade, 91
Shaw, Vero, 24
Shoulder, 70
Show demeanour, 146
Show preparation, 142
Shows, 157
Silver Melody, Ch., 54
Singleton, W. M., 38, 43
Size, 59, 61
Skerne Scotch Lass, 55
Skull, 60, 63
Skye Terrier, 20
Sleeping boxes, 84, 145
Smith, Chas. H., 19
Snookers Double, 35
South of England Scottish Terrier
 Club, 30
Specialist Clubs, 59
Spelman, W. W., 27
Spine, 75
Splinter II, 24, 46
Spofford Dauntless Laddie, Ch., 30, 49
Standard of the breed, 24, 59, 167
Stifle (knee joint), 63
Stonehenge, 20
Stop, 63
Strain, 111
Stricture, 139
Stripping, 147
Stripping knife, 149
Stud-cards, 141
Stud dog, 137
Stud visits, 116
Sunray, Ch., 46
Syringa, Ch., 26, 52

T

Tail, 25, 59
Tail-female, 46
Tail-male, 46
Talavera Toddler, Ch., 54
Tartan, 24
Tattenham kennel, 50
Teeth, 68
Teething, 134
Temperament, 24, 110, 142

Temperature, 178
Thermometer, 179
Thigh, 73
Thinning-scissors, 151
Thorpe, Miss D. I., 40
Toe-nails, 105
Tone of voice, 100
Training, 97
Training to lead, 101
Trimming, 147
Tweburn Clincher, Ch., 78
Tweed, H. R. B., 29, 57
Twinkle of Docken, 50
Type, 111

U

Undercliffe Rosie, 52
Undercoat, 76

V

Viewpark kennel, 17

W

Wall-pens, 85
Walsing kennel, 38 et seq.
Waterford Wagtail, 50
Weight, 61
Wenbury Westpark Superman, Ch., 53
West Highland White Terrier, 20, 62
Western Highlands, 20
Westpark kennel, 44 et seq.
Whelping, 116
Whelping-box, 118
Wilforths Wat-a-Lass, Ch., 50
Withers, 71
Worms (in adults), 182
Worms (in puppies), 132
Worry, 24
Writtle Patricia, Ch., 49
Wyrebury kennel, 44 et seq.

X

X-ray, 121

Y

Yorkshire Terrier, 20